A Name Unbroken

D1374131

A Name Unbroken

Michael Mason

THE AZRIELI FOUNDATION
www.azrielifoundation.org

Cover and book design by Mark Goldstein
Endpaper maps by Martin Gilbert
Map on page xxvii by François Blanc

LIBRARY AND ARCHIVES CANADA CATALOGUING IN PUBLICATION

Mason, Michael, 1928–, author
    A name unbroken/ Michael Mason.

(The Azrieli series of holocaust survivor memoirs; 7)
Includes index.
ISBN 978-1-897470-56-5 (paperback)

1. Mason, Michael, 1928–. 2. Holocaust, Jewish (1939–1945) – Hungary – Personal narratives. 3. World War, 1939–1945 – Conscript labor – Germany – Seeshaupt – Biography. 4. Jews – Hungary – Biography. 5. Holocaust survivors – Canada – Biography. I. Azrieli Foundation, issuing body II. Title.

DS135.H93M38 2015   940.53'18092   C2015-905988-7

MIX
From responsible sources
FSC   FSC® C004191
www.fsc.org

PRINTED IN CANADA

The Azrieli Series of Holocaust Survivor Memoirs

Naomi Azrieli, Publisher

Jody Spiegel, Program Director
Arielle Berger, Managing Editor
Elizabeth Lasserre, Senior Editor, French-Language Editions
Farla Klaiman, Editor
Elin Beaumont, Senior Educational Outreach and Events Coordinator
Catherine Person, Educational Outreach and Events Coordinator,
    Quebec and French Canada
Marc-Olivier Cloutier, Educational Outreach and Events Assistant,
    Quebec and French Canada
Tim MacKay, Digital Platform Manager
Elizabeth Banks, Digital Asset and Archive Curator
Susan Roitman, Office Manager (Toronto)
Mary Mellas, Executive Assistant and Human Resources (Montreal)

Mark Goldstein, Art Director
François Blanc, Cartographer
Bruno Paradis, Layout, French-language editions

Contents

Series Preface:
In their own words...

In telling these stories, the writers have liberated themselves. For so many years we did not speak about it, even when we became free people living in a free society. Now, when at last we are writing about what happened to us in this dark period of history, knowing that our stories will be read and live on, it is possible for us to feel truly free. These unique historical documents put a face on what was lost, and allow readers to grasp the enormity of what happened to six million Jews – one story at a time.

David J. Azrieli, C.M., C.Q., M.Arch
Holocaust survivor and founder, The Azrieli Foundation

Since the end of World War ii, over 30,000 Jewish Holocaust survivors have immigrated to Canada. Who they are, where they came from, what they experienced and how they built new lives for themselves and their families are important parts of our Canadian heritage. The Azrieli Foundation's Holocaust Survivor Memoirs Program was established to preserve and share the memoirs written by those who survived the twentieth-century Nazi genocide of the Jews of Europe and later made their way to Canada. The program is guided by the conviction that each survivor of the Holocaust has a remarkable story to tell, and that such stories play an important role in education about tolerance and diversity.

Millions of individual stories are lost to us forever. By preserving the stories written by survivors and making them widely available to a broad audience, the Azrieli Foundation's Holocaust Survivor Memoirs Program seeks to sustain the memory of all those who perished at the hands of hatred, abetted by indifference and apathy. The personal accounts of those who survived against all odds are as different as the people who wrote them, but all demonstrate the courage, strength, wit and luck that it took to prevail and survive in such terrible adversity. The memoirs are also moving tributes to people – strangers and friends – who risked their lives to help others, and who, through acts of kindness and decency in the darkest of moments, frequently helped the persecuted maintain faith in humanity and courage to endure. These accounts offer inspiration to all, as does the survivors' desire to share their experiences so that new generations can learn from them.

The Holocaust Survivor Memoirs Program collects, archives and publishes these distinctive records and the print editions are available free of charge to educational institutions and Holocaust-education programs across Canada. They are also available for sale to the general public at bookstores. All revenues to the Azrieli Foundation from the sales of the Azrieli Series of Holocaust Survivor Memoirs go toward the publishing and educational work of the memoirs program.

∽

The Azrieli Foundation would like to express appreciation to the following people for their invaluable efforts in producing this book: Doris Bergen, Sherry Dodson (Maracle Press), Therese Parent, Allegra Robinson, and Margie Wolfe and Emma Rodgers of Second Story Press.

About the Glossary

The following memoir contains a number of terms, concepts and historical references that may be unfamiliar to the reader. For information on major organizations; significant historical events and people; geographical locations; religious and cultural terms; and foreign-language words and expressions that will help give context and background to the events described in the text, please see the glossary beginning on page 113.

Introduction

Although Michael Mason was living in Budapest when Nazi Germany occupied Hungary in March 1944, his family was not originally from the Hungarian capital. They came from farther north, in the region of Carpatho-Ruthenia that was part of either Hungary or Czechoslovakia, depending on the precise location of the border that moved a number of times during the first half of the twentieth century. Michael was born in Beregszász – where Jews made up around one third of the population – when the city was part of Czechoslovakia as a result of the post-World War I settlement that saw Hungary lose close to two-thirds of its territory and over half its population. As a young boy, he moved with his family to the Hungarian border town of Sátoraljaújhely. The memoir gives the sense that his father – like many Hungarian Jews – was a proud "Magyar" who had fought during World War I for the multi-ethnic Austro-Hungarian Empire. In 1941, the family was on the move again – this time to Budapest. As Michael explains, this move to the capital was a response to the worsening economic situation his father faced as a result of the anti-Jewish laws implemented in the late 1930s.

Hungarian Jews were subjected to an increasingly intrusive legal attack across the interwar years, which were dominated by a series of right-wing governments under the Regent Miklós Horthy. In the early 1920s, a *numerus clausus* that set a quota on Jewish university enrollment was enacted although ultimately never fully enforced. In the late 1930s, however, the "First Jewish Law" and "Second Jewish Law" placed limits on Jewish participation in the economy, professions and administration. This economic attack on Jews affected Michael's father, who was forced to sell his tavern. Many Hungarian survivors who were children at the time remember these years as ones when their fathers lost their jobs and the family suffered increasing economic hardship. A further attack came in 1941 when the Hungarian state enacted the third in this series of anti-Jewish laws. Paralleling the Nuremberg Laws enacted in Nazi Germany, this legislation prohibited marriage and sexual relations between Jews and non-Jews.

However, even as restrictions were being implemented, Hungarian Jews were seen to be living in something of an island of relative safety during the early 1940s compared to the Jewish communities in the countries around them. This was perhaps all the more surprising given that Hungary had become an ally of Nazi Germany in November 1940, largely with a view to regaining territory lost in the aftermath of World War I. These aims of territorial enlargement were successful, with border regions such as those that Michael was originally from coming back under Hungarian control. During the early 1940s, Hungary was seen to be something of a reluctant ally as far as solving the so-called "Jewish question" went. Admiral Horthy rejected German demands for wholesale deportations. The argument of the Hungarian state was that Jews were already being dealt with by the laws that the state had enacted, and were too central to the Hungarian military economy to be removed en masse.

In March 1944, everything changed when Germany invaded its somewhat reluctant ally. How far this occupation was triggered by the existence of a large extant national Jewish community in 1944 and how far by Hungarian attempts to extricate themselves from the war remains a debate among historians. Whatever the reason, the occupation meant a dramatic change in fortunes for Hungarian Jews, Michael's family among them. It was, as Michael remembers, a rather unusual occupation. Writing of the events of March 19, 1944, Michael describes a "friendly" occupation, with German troops in Budapest looking "more like a parade than an occupation force." His comments are significant. The occupying forces in Hungary were tiny, although they did include Adolf Eichmann. The rapid implementation of anti-Jewish measures in the aftermath of the German occupation depended on Hungarian collaboration at all levels – from the newly appointed government of former ambassador to Berlin Döme Sztójay, through the Interior Ministry and its triad of new appointees – Andor Jaross, László Baky and László Endre – to regional and local authorities and the rural gendarmes and urban police. Although the question of how "German" or "Hungarian" the Holocaust in Hungary was remains very much a live one among historians, politicians and the public in Hungary, it does seem clear from the research undertaken in the last couple of decades that the scale of the attack on Hungarian Jews owed much to opportunism on the part of significant elements of the Hungarian state and society, fuelled by a desire for economic enrichment at the Jews' expense.

The events of the spring and summer of 1944, in the immediate aftermath of the German occupation, are shocking because of the rapidity and lateness with which this "last chapter" of the Holocaust was carried out. There were only fifty-six days between the occupation and the first deportations to the camps. Over the next fifty-six days, more or less the entire Jewish population outside of the capital – over 400,000 people, Michael among them – was deported, the vast majority to Auschwitz-Birkenau. The familiar elements of the Holocaust – marking with a yellow star, concentrating into ghettos, deportation to camps – that took place across several years in Poland were telescoped into a few bloody months in the late spring and early summer of 1944.

Michael was caught up in the mass deportations, taken to the brickyard in Monor that served as one of the entrainment points and deported from there to Auschwitz-Birkenau in early July 1944.

In many ways, it was a mistake that he ended up on the deportation train that headed north from Monor and on to Auschwitz. As Michael suggests in his memoir, it appears to have been a local official particularly keen to do his job who ensured that Michael, and other boys called up to work on the land, were included in the sweep that made the area *Judenfrei*. The remainder of his family, living in Budapest, were spared deportation as a result of the decision of the Hungarian Regent, Miklós Horthy, to halt deportations before they reached the capital. Also spared from deportation was another group that Michael refers to in a number of places in his memoir – Jewish men serving in labour battalions.

When Hungary first entered the war, Jewish men were called up alongside non-Jewish men for military service. Jewish men between the ages of twenty and forty-two were not put into armed units, but rather labour battalions that served alongside armed units on the Eastern front. Here they suffered harsh conditions, in some cases attacks by antisemitic officers, and very high casualty rates. In 1944, younger and older men were called up into labour battalions. Older teenagers and middle aged men in their forties were being called up into labour service, including, in some cases, out of the ghettos, which led to conflict between different branches of the Hungarian state. Michael was just a few years too young to be called up into these units.

The call-up of Jewish men from 1941 onwards and then a renewed and extended call-up in 1944 meant that adult Jewish men and Jewish women tended to have quite different experiences. Looking through the existing lists from ghettos in western Hungary, I have been struck time and time again by how much women, children and the elderly predominate. The trains that took Jews from Hungary – including Michael – to Auschwitz-Birkenau in the late spring and early summer of 1944 were packed with women, children and the elderly. The absence of Jewish men in their upper teens, twenties and thirties explains why the death rate on arrival was so high during the Hungarian deportations. Michael – who claimed to be an eighteen-year-old farmer – was one of those selected for labour on arrival. However, the vast majority of those deported from Hungary were selected for immediate gassing. Michael shows himself sensitive to the importance of age to survival. As he reflects at the close of his memoir, "If I had been a couple of years younger or older, I probably would not have survived," noting that, "a couple of years younger, I would not have gotten past the selections in Auschwitz." Age mattered. But in the Hungarian case in particular, gender also did.

Just as marked in Hungary is how geography mattered. Michael was, in many ways, in the wrong place at the wrong time. If he had been back home in Budapest, rather than working on the land in Monor, he would have been spared deportation to Auschwitz in the summer of 1944 and would have had a very different wartime story. The thirty kilometres between Budapest and Monor were a distance that resulted in very different outcomes. Deportations from Hungary took place on a zonal basis, broadly moving from east, through the south of the country, to the west, with Budapest's Jews scheduled to be the final community transported out of the country. The Jews from Michael's birthplace – Beregszász – were among the first deported from Hungary in the second half of May 1944. The Jews from Michael's childhood town, Sátoraljaújhely, were deported during the same period in May, with the last group deported on June 3, 1944. Michael was deported from Monor in early July 1944. He was sent to Auschwitz just at the moment that Horthy decided to halt the deportations as a result of both domestic and international pressure and the broader context of the changing shape of the war during 1944.

But that is not to say that Jews in Budapest escaped completely by dint of living in the capital. As Michael's memoir suggests, the rest of his family who lived in Budapest were exposed to, and sought to escape from, a range of different threats across 1944. Jews in Budapest, like elsewhere in the country, had to wear the yellow star on outer clothing and were concentrated in ghettos during June 1944. The shape of the ghetto in Budapest in the summer and fall of 1944 was rather unusual. Jews lived in close to 2,000 apartment buildings spread throughout the entire city rather than a single fenced ghetto. They were free to leave these buildings to shop or visit sick relatives in hospital for only a few hours per day – the curfew hours that Michael refers to.

During the late summer of 1944, conditions improved somewhat for Budapest Jews. After the halting of deportations there was something of a lull, in particular in the aftermath of a new and more moderate government led by General Géza Lakatos. However, things changed dramatically in mid-October, after Horthy was removed by the Germans following a bungled attempt to withdraw from the war. A new puppet government was installed on October 15, headed by the leader of the native fascist Nyilas – or Arrow Cross – party, Ferenc Szálasi. Deportations of Jews commenced from Budapest, although this time on foot in so-called death marches and towards Austria rather than Auschwitz.

These changed circumstances in Budapest are the backdrop to the actions of someone whom Michael's parents credit with their survival, and whom Michael became an advocate for in post-war Canada: Raoul Wallenberg. Plenty of mythology surrounds Raoul Wallenberg, including, for example, the number of Jews in Budapest that he saved during the second half of 1944 and first weeks of 1945. When he first arrived in Budapest in July 1944, Wallenberg was part of a bigger team in the Swedish embassy that negotiated with the Hungarian government to gain permission to issue up to 4,500 Swedish protective passports. In reality the number of protective documents issued was far, far greater, reaching perhaps three to four times this figure. Most were called *Schutzpässe*, giving proof that individuals were under Swedish embassy protection until the point when they were able to travel to Sweden. Those receiving this paperwork were supposed to have at least some connection with Sweden although, in practice, these relationships were often vague or indeed non-existent. As Michael suggests, his mother managed to get hold of these papers for her family, who had no obvious Swedish links. The Swedish embassy were not the only ones – nor indeed the first ones – to produce protective documents in Budapest. Carl Lutz, vice-consul of the Swiss embassy, was also very active in issuing paperwork in the summer of 1944 and in housing Jews in protected buildings, including the so-called Glass House on Vadász Street. Other neutral powers and organizations became involved in these rescue activities.

Given the context of war and occupation, the possibilities of travel to Sweden – or other neutral countries – were effectively nil. Therefore, during July and August 1944, the neutral powers began discussing plans to protect Jews with bricks and mortar and not simply paperwork. In September, it seemed that these plans had been shelved, for the time being at least. However, in October, following the Arrow Cross rise to power, plans to provide separate housing for protected Jews were implemented. For the Arrow Cross government, there was a sense of diplomatic credibility gained through negotiating with the neutral powers. Therefore, when plans were unveiled over what to do with Jews remaining in the country, six categories – each receiving separate treatment – were identified, one of which was Jews under foreign protection. Rather than living in apartment buildings spread throughout the city, Jews remaining in Budapest were concentrated into two ghettos at the end of November. Jews without protective papers who remained in the capital were to move to a fenced ghetto established in the heart of the traditional Jewish quarter in the seventh district of Pest. Jews with protective papers were to move into a loose collection of around 120 apartment buildings scattered over a small number of streets in Újlipótváros district, close to Margaret Island. Here they were not safe, but were at risk of being rounded up by Arrow Cross gangs, marched to the Danube and shot into the river. The memorial that marks this makeshift execution site in the very heart of the city is one that Michael writes of visiting when he returned to Budapest after his retirement.

What Raoul Wallenberg did during this chaotic period remains hard to say with certainty. I think that historian Paul Levine is probably right to conclude that "most of what Wallenberg did between October 15 and January 17 remained similar to what he had been doing. The situations which continued to dominate his time and consume his energy were less a matter of confrontation on the street, at railway yards or on the Danube's quay, and more of the quieter business of negotiations with Hungarian and sometimes German officials."[1] It was a case, he suggests, of "the continuing importance" of what he terms "bureaucratic resistance" rather than acts of individual heroism.[2] Wallenberg's emergence as a heroic figure in the post-war world owed as much to his disappearance in mid-January 1945, when he crossed the front lines to negotiate with the Soviets, as it did to his rescue activities in the second half of 1944. The story of Wallenberg's disappearance into the Soviet prison system is one that occupied Michael's attention during the 1980s, when Wallenberg became something of a *cause célèbre* in Cold War North America in particular.

Throwing himself into the campaign to find out the truth about Wallenberg's Soviet imprisonment, Michael was responding first and foremost to a character central to his father's story rather than his own. While his father was in Budapest and other family members were in hiding or lying low, Michael was a slave labourer in the continental-wide camp system. Selected for labour at Auschwitz as a teenage boy, Michael was among those Hungarian Jews quickly moved into the wartime slave labour economy. He, like others, was sent west, ending up in Germany at the camp of Mühldorf – a subcamp of Dachau – where he worked to clear a forest for the construction of an aircraft factory. This moment in the second half of 1944 when Michael found himself in a labour camp in Germany is striking. Just a few years before, Germany had been made *Judenfrei* as Jews were sent to the ghettos in the east. However, in an ultimately fruitless attempt

1   Paul A. Levine, *Raoul Wallenberg in Budapest. Myth, History and Holocaust* (London: Vallentine Mitchell, 2010) pp. 291–2.
2   Levine, *Raoul Wallenberg in Budapest*, p. 307.

to win the war, Jews were being deployed to Germany to undertake what in most cases remained unfinished construction projects. Thousands of Hungarian Jewish young men and women – including Michael – were deployed to camps and subcamps across Germany. There, as Michael himself became aware of when clearing up rubble after an air raid in March 1945, it became increasingly evident that the war was slowly coming to an end. Michael was ultimately liberated on German soil when he and other prisoners were hurriedly evacuated from the camp in a last-gasp attempt to keep prisoners from the advancing Allied forces.

Michael, in writing of just under a year surviving slave labour, gives rich insight into the nature and variety of work undertaken by prisoners like him. It becomes clear that two factors were of considerable importance. Firstly, it mattered what kind of work you were undertaking – specifically in terms of the physical toll it took on your emaciated body. Secondly, and something that played a critical role in determining the kind of work you undertook, it mattered just who your foreman or overseer was. Slave labour was neither a monolithic nor a homogenous experience. The value of memoirs such as this is that it allows us to understand the particularities of what forced labour meant for one man and the ways that he sought to navigate his way through the labour camp system. Survivor memoirs like Michael's not only humanize the narrative, but also develop the narrative by providing a glimpse into a lived experience.

But Michael's memoir is important not only because of the insights it provides into a Hungarian Jewish teenager seeking to survive the Holocaust. It is also rich in the details of his post-war life. From an emotional return home to knock on his apartment door to see if anyone else from his family had survived, to his early life in post-war Hungary and then Canada, Michael writes of the challenges of rebuilding life after the Holocaust. Michael sought to think about the future rather than the past, and avoided talking directly about the Holocaust. As he explains in his preface, he decided not to discuss his wartime experiences with his children, but only began to speak and write about the Holocaust later in life to ensure that his grand-children's generation was made aware of the events that he had lived through.

However, while it is apparent that Michael – through this mem-oir and his starting to talk to students about his life – has assumed a more vocal survivor identity, he was never silent in the decades be-fore. His identification with the cause of Raoul Wallenberg is telling; it was one that he took up fully and played a leading national role in. Reflecting on Michael's own immersion into lobbying on behalf of Wallenberg, I wonder if this was as much about Michael's self-identi-fication with Wallenberg as a fellow-prisoner as it was about his iden-tification with Wallenberg as a critical player in his family's story of survival. Although Michael may not have written or spoken about the Holocaust until relatively recently, I would suggest that he has been acting in response to the Holocaust and its legacy for far longer.

Tim Cole
University of Bristol
2015

FURTHER READING

Braham, Randolph L. *The Politics of Genocide: The Holocaust in Hungary* (New York: Columbia University Press, 1994)

Cole, Tim. *Holocaust City: The Making of a Jewish Ghetto* (New York: Routledge, 2003)

Cole, Tim. *Traces of the Holocaust: Journeying in and out of the Ghettos* (London: Continuum, 2011)

Gerlach, Christian, and Götz Aly. *Das letzte Kapitel: Realpolitik, Ideologie und der Mord an den ungarischen Juden 1944/1945* (Stuttgart München: Deutsche Verlags-Anstalt, 2002)

Levine, Paul A. *Raoul Wallenberg in Budapest. Myth, History and Holocaust* (London: Vallentine Mitchell, 2010)

Vági, Zoltán, László Csősz and Gábor Kádár. *The Holocaust in Hungary: Evolution of a Genocide* (Plymouth: AltaMira Press in association with the United States Holocaust Memorial Museum, 2013)

Map

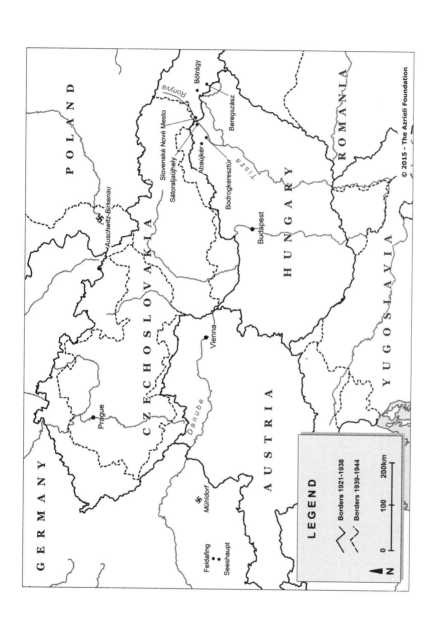

GERMANY

POLAND

CZECHOSLOVAKIA

AUSTRIA

HUNGARY

ROMANIA

YUGOSLAVIA

Auschwitz-Birkenau

Prague

Danube

Mühldorf

Feldafing

Seeshaupt

Vienna

Budapest

Slovenské Nové Mesto

Sátoraljaújhely

Abaújkér

Bodrogkeresztúr

Tisza

Ronyva

Bótrágy

Beregszász

LEGEND

Borders 1921-1938

Borders 1939-1944

0   100   200km

N

I dedicate this book to the memory of my parents, Ferencz and Gisel Friedman, to my late wife, Ruth (Ricky), and to our late son, Andrew.

To my wife, Doreen, and our children, Robin, Tov, Roseanne, Cheryl and Joel.

To our grandchildren, Sarah Rachel, Danielle, Andrew, Zoe, Sophie, Adam, Jacob, Emily, Ruby, Henry, Selma, Cy and Av.

Author's Preface

On a beautiful summer evening, as the sun set over Lake Simcoe, I sat on the cottage deck watching the last rays shining over the water. As I picked up my camera to take a picture of a sailboat illuminated in the water, my thoughts suddenly jumped back to the day when, as a young immigrant, I landed in Canada. Back then, I would have never believed that some day I would be watching such a beautiful sight from my own country house. I looked behind me to where my grandchildren were playing and thought back to my own childhood in Hungary. My grandson Andrew came over and asked me what I was thinking about. I said, "I am thinking about what I was doing when I was your age. Someday I will write it all down, and when you get older, I will let you read it."

But how could I tell this beautiful young boy how I lived through the murder of the Jewish people? Six million. The Holocaust was the worst atrocity ever committed. I was just fifteen years old when I was taken to Poland, to the Auschwitz death camp. As a teenager, I had little understanding of the hatred that religion can inspire against human beings. Living in the democratic country of Canada, even I would find it hard to believe that civilized people could have done what the Nazis did to the European Jews. I tried to bring my thoughts back to the present so as not to spoil the children's time.

When my first child was born, I was determined to never speak

2 A NAME UNBROKEN

about the time I spent in the Nazi camps. I did not want my children to grow up with the trauma of what had happened to most of our family in Europe. I lost a brother, nine uncles and aunts, and twenty-eight cousins during the war.

On my seventy-fifth birthday, I decided that it was finally time to keep my promise to my grandson and begin writing about my childhood and my life.

First Ventures

My father met my mother by chance. He was from Abaújkér in northern Hungary and she lived about a hundred and fifty kilometres away in a small village called Bótrágy (now called Batrad'), which was part of Czechoslovakia at the time she was born, and is now in Ukraine. My father, Ferencz Friedman, was in the logging business and had gone to Košice, a city in Czechoslovakia, to visit a friend. There, he noticed a photo of his friend's wife with another girl. He thought this girl was beautiful and asked his friend who she was. He said that her name was Gisel Weisz and that she was single. Even though my father was engaged to be married – a matchmaker had arranged a marriage to a girl he had seen only once – he asked for Gisel's address and immediately went to visit her. It was love at first sight for both of them. Two months later, they were married.

My maternal grandmother, Regina, was unhappy about the marriage because her family was Hasidic and my father was not as religious as they were.[1] My mother was the youngest of seven children. Behind her family's house, which was the biggest in the village, my grandfather Jacob had built both a synagogue and a mikvah. My

---

1   For information on Hasidic Judaism, as well as on other religious, historical and cultural terms; significant historical events and people; geographical locations; major organizations; and foreign-language words and expressions contained in the text, please see the glossary.

grandparents owned two other properties; there was a small Jewish cemetery behind one of them and another was a farm, where he hired labourers to work. Unfortunately, at the age of thirty-five, my grandfather had a heart attack; he died before I was born in 1928.

After my parents got married, they moved to the city of Beregszász and my father started a business selling building materials. Beregszász, which is now called Berehove, was a small city in Czechoslovakia seventy-five kilometres from the Hungarian border, so everybody in the city spoke Hungarian. Father used to say that it showed how much he was in love with Mother that he agreed to live outside of Hungary. He was a great Hungarian nationalist and had been a Hussar in the army, part of the cavalry. I've seen photos of him on horseback holding a sword and wearing a well-decorated uniform.

At some point during the interwar period in Czechoslovakia, the government required all Hungarians to take out Czechoslovakian citizenship. My father refused, so we had to leave the country. We had a large family, and moving was not easy. I had just started public school and my older brother, Laci, and sister, Magda, attended different schools. My younger brother, Fredi, had just been born. One of my earliest memories is of this move across the border into Hungary. The train ride to the border was exciting, but when the Hungarian customs officers gave my father a hard time, I decided that I did not like Hungarians.

My father was the ultimate businessman – at just thirty years old he had already owned three different businesses. He started out as a textile dealer, later purchased a logging company in the Carpathian mountains, and then worked in building materials. In our new home, the border city of Sátoraljaújhely, my father purchased a tavern and we moved into the house above it. The tavern was on the edge of the city, which was good for business because when farmers came to the city they all stopped in for a drink and breakfast. My father also owned a small property across the street, as well as a cow and a barn. A family lived there to look after the place, and the cow provided us with milk. The cow went out with a herd every morning to graze and came home every evening, but it would not go to the stable without stopping at the tavern door to receive a slice of bread. People often came to see the cow walking up the tavern's front steps, waiting for the bread.

Down the street from us was the small Ronyva River that marked the border with Czechoslovakia. On one end of the bridge over the river stood a Hungarian soldier; on the other, a Czech soldier. After World War I, the Treaty of Trianon had given a portion of the town, as part of Hungary's northern territories, to Czechoslovakia. There was constant animosity between the two countries.

Alongside the river, the Roma, then called gypsies, lived in mud houses. My father employed some Roma as musicians at the tavern, and I made friends with some of their boys. Well, sometimes we were friends and sometimes we fought, but I loved to spend time with them. The Roma were different from many of my Jewish friends, who spent their time studying, and I learned a lot of things from them that I never told my parents. We would catch small fish in the river, make a fire, put the fish on sticks and fry and eat them. My new friends had no rules or specific bedtimes given to them by their parents. I, on the other hand, had strict rules around what I was allowed to do.

One Shabbat after lunch, one of my gypsy friends, Joska, who was a year older than me, asked me to go with him up the mountain to kill a wild pig. I asked my father for permission. He was snoozing on the couch and he murmured something that I thought meant yes, so off we went. I was carrying my short walking stick that had a tiny hatchet at the end as a handle, and Joska brought a small pocket knife. With these in hand, we were planning to kill this supposed wild pig. Of course, no wild pig was caught. We got back very late. As we approached our tavern, we saw a crowd of people out front with lanterns. We asked what was happening and were told that a little boy must have fallen in the river and they were planning to drag it. I realized that was for me. When I walked into the tavern, everyone hugged and kissed me, but afterward, I got a beating from my mother. My father never punished us physically. A look from him was enough to make us feel bad.

I was about twelve years old when Joska invited me to come along to steal some corn and fruit from the farmers' fields. We built a fire and roasted the stolen corn, and I thought it was the tastiest I had ever eaten. I was always ready for anything; my brother Laci was happier to read a book and seldom came with us. Joska also showed me how to "borrow" bicycles and go for joy rides. When someone rode up to a store and went inside, we took his bike and went for a spin. When we tired of it we dropped the bike where the owner would likely find it. Joska explained that this way, the owner could not say it was stolen, only misplaced. One day, he told me that you could not be friends with girls once they developed breasts because they became sissies, and then they were only good for having babies. He went on to tell me about how babies are made and said I should try it. I didn't know anything about sex and I did not believe what he was telling me, so he offered his sister to me to learn. I was offended and hit him, and then he got mad and really beat me. I had to tell my mother that I had fallen. I complained about the beating to the gypsy community's leader. He sat us down and explained about the birds and the bees using plain language. The way he explained it, I do not think my mother would have approved.

When I was growing up, Újhely, as we used to call it, had a population of about 13,000, of which about 4,000 were Jewish. The Jews were mainly Conservative in their religious beliefs and most of them kept the Sabbath, or Shabbat. My family was modern Orthodox. My father sent us to cheder after school, but our teacher was satisfied if we learned only a little, and let us out to play instead. We went to synagogue on Shabbat and my mother always had a *Shabbat goy* attend to the household needs while we observed the rules of the Sabbath. Every Friday, we took our *cholent* stew to the bakery, where it cooked overnight, and we picked it up after Shabbat morning services. Our small synagogue, which thirty or forty families belonged to, was across from the bakery.

One morning, while I was walking to synagogue with my brother Laci, we saw a 100-forint note on the sidewalk. It was a large amount of money, and we were debating what to do because you are not supposed to touch money on Shabbat. But it was more money than we had ever had. Against my wishes, we decided to use our shoes to push it to the edge of the sidewalk and then cover it with a small stone. After Shabbat was over we ran to get it but it was gone. I blamed my brother for the loss – he was more religious than I was. We both, however, thought that God was watching us and that if we committed a sin, it would be recorded somewhere. At the end of the Jewish year, on the holiday of Yom Kippur, it is said that you will be punished for the sins you have committed during the year. I started to doubt this on one Yom Kippur, which is the day of fasting. We were playing outside and I forgot I was not supposed to drink water. Nothing happened when I did. I had expected that if not God, then an angel would be sent to punish me.

When I was about twelve, my schoolteacher taught us how silk was made from cocoons: the worms eat the leaves of mulberry trees and when they get big enough, they wrap themselves in their saliva, which forms into the cocoon. After the worms unwind the cocoons, the thread is the silk. After the lesson, the teacher promoted silk-making as a way to make a lot of money and help our country. The government provided instructions and the larva, and my brother Laci and I went into business. We had a big mulberry tree in our backyard and we thought its leaves would be enough to feed the worms. We picked all the leaves off our tree, but those hungry worms weren't even a quarter of the size they should have grown. We hired gypsy kids to pick more leaves and I think they cleaned the leaves off every tree in the neighbourhood. My father was not very pleased about advancing us money to pay the kids. Finally, the cocoons formed and we packaged and shipped them to the promoter. We received a con-

siderably large amount of money, for our hungry worms had produced first-rate cocoons. This was my first financial venture.

We had a peaceful, happy childhood, and never expected what
was to come. Jews were accepted in Hungary as citizens. They owned
properties, businesses and factories. Although only a limited number of Jews were accepted in the universities, and a Jew could not sell
cigarettes or tobacco unless the government allowed it, my father's
army career as a Hussar gave him the privilege and permission to sell
liquor and cigarettes.

I didn't feel as though antisemitism was all that out in the open.
Even though I often heard people say, "I am going to the Jew store," I
also heard, "I only go to the Jewish doctor or lawyer because they are
the best." Although a Jewish person wasn't allowed to belong to any
high society group, Hungarians were always ready to say they had a
Jewish friend.

At the tavern, my father employed a bouncer, a man named Gyula.
He was a tough guy, muscular, though not tall. As a sometimes smug-
gler and thief, he was always in some kind of trouble. However, my
father liked and trusted him. One day, a man came into the tavern,
sat at the bar and ordered a drink. He started to talk about Jews, saying things like, "They are robbing us blind. We should throw them
out." My father responded, "Finish your drink and get out of here."
The man pulled out a dagger and slammed it into the bar, yelling, "No
f***ing Jew is going to tell me to get out!" Gyula pulled the guy out
of his chair and beat him badly. He then grabbed the guy's wallet out
of his pocket, took enough to cover the damage to the bar and threw
him out. About an hour later, the guy appeared with a police officer,
who asked what had happened. Gyula told the officer the man had
been thrown out and the policeman, winking at Gyula, said that both
of them would be arrested for disturbing the peace. Walking out, the
officer asked Gyula, "How much time do you need to teach this guy
a lesson? He replied, "Ten minutes will be enough." The officer took
both of them to jail, put them in the same cell and let Gyula out after

ten minutes. In that time, Gyula beat him some more. The police kept the guy for two more days to cool off; they liked Gyula because he was an occasional informer.

In the winter, we always experienced shortages of everything – especially coal for heating or any other fuel – so it was more difficult to buy these things. When my father mentioned to Gyula that we were running out of coal, we found our coal bin full the next morning. Gyula confided to me that there was a boxcar full of coal outside of the railway station that was not being used. His approach was: why not give to those who need? He liked me and taught me things that my parents would not have approved of, had they known. He also always liked our maids, young girls from the countryside. I knew that he climbed through the window at night to visit the girls.

One day a detective came into our tavern and told my father, "I know that the Jewish people keep in touch with each other, even over the border. I am sure that you know the Jewish shoe store in Slovenské Nové Mesto, across the river. I see that you are wearing nice Bata shoes. I like them too, my size is forty-four and I prefer black." Then he walked out. Bata shoes were made in Czechoslovakia and we could not get them in our town. My father knew that was an order and that if he wanted police protection, he should do what he could. He asked Gyula to go across the river and get him a pair of shoes. Gyula asked me if I wanted to go with him and naturally I said yes.

We went to the river and crawled under the bridge to the other side. We bought the shoes and had just managed to crawl back when a police officer saw us and started to chase us. Just across from our tavern was a yard where huge cement sewer pipes were stored. We ducked into the yard, slipped into one of the pipes and stayed hidden for about an hour before we dared to come out. Gyula charged my father more for the shoes than they had cost him, and he also charged for the smuggling. He explained to me that is how you have to think, to take advantage of opportunities. Another time, we "borrowed" a bike that was outside the tavern. Later, when he returned it, he told me that you have to help yourself, that nobody will look after you if you do not look after yourself. Little did I know then that all his teaching would later help save my life.

In school, before Easter, the gentile kids always said to us, "You Jews killed Jesus." That was their upbringing, having heard this from the priests in church. On Easter, the sermon in Catholic churches was often an incitement against the Jews, as Christ-killers. The priests never mentioned that Christ lived and died as a Jew. So the Easter holiday was usually a bad time for Jews – people were beaten, sometimes even killed. One year, one of the musicians told my father that people were planning a pogrom on Easter evening after the church service. My father knew that could also mean stealing and breaking into Jewish stores. Before that evening, Gyula and the bartender came over to our house and offered to stay with us to protect us from harm. We turned off the lights, my father picked up a fire iron and Gyula and the bartender guarded our windows with heavy wooden sticks. Luckily, we were not attacked, but some of our neighbours were. Our Jewish grocery store was broken into and a lot of stock was taken; the counters were smashed and the whole store suffered damage. My father and us boys went over to help clean up the mess. The police did nothing. From experience, we knew it was useless to complain.

In the newspapers, we read about the anti-Jewish situation in Germany, which started to influence the Hungarian government and population. The Hungarians were allies with Germany. In our schools, the atmosphere was growing more antisemitic. Even the teachers instigated anti-Jewish sentiment. For a couple of months in Grade 8, I was out of school because my left leg had become crippled and the doctors were having a hard time diagnosing what was wrong. When it finally got better and I went back to school, my teacher, Mr. Lovas, said, "What was the matter, the Red Sea did not swallow you?" I told him that Moses was strong and held it back for me. He called me an arrogant Jew and punished me. Our gentile classmates' attitudes changed as well, and more fights took place between Jewish and gentile boys. My older brother, Laci, was more of a scholar than a fighter, and my friends and I often had to fight to protect him from abuse. I was taken to the principal's office for fighting on several occasions. Sometimes we were chased from school all the way home. We would build a pile of stones behind our gate, quickly grab some, turn on our attackers and chase them back.

One Friday evening, coming home from Erev Shabbat services, my father invited a Polish-Jewish man for dinner. He spoke Yiddish, which I could understand because I had learned it from my parents. We spoke Hungarian at home, but when my parents didn't want us to understand them, they spoke Yiddish to each other; it didn't take me long to be able to understand them. Also, in school I studied German, which is similar to Yiddish. During dinner, our guest told us to run from Hungary, that we would be killed next, just like the Polish Jews were being killed. He said, "You still have time; go now!" After he left, my mother said, "The Polish Jews are always suffering from pogroms and killings. Here in Hungary, we are relatively safe."

In May 1938 and May 1939, the Hungarian government had introduced new laws against the Jewish population, reducing the number of Jews allowed to practise in certain professions, such as law and medicine. One law took away Jews' rights to have business licences, which were needed to sell liquor or cigarettes. This law forced my father to sell the tavern, though he stayed on as a paid employee. A man who had been a noble Austro-Hungarian prince, expelled from the family for marrying a Hungarian peasant woman, was the new owner. He was no businessman – his wife did all the work, cooking and looking after their property. They lived on the mountain and he spent his time reading, walking and playing with his two cats. In the tavern he just sat and smoked his cigar. This arrangement lasted for a little while, but eventually, in 1941, we moved to the capital city of Budapest. My father hoped for better economic opportunities there. I was thirteen years old when I continued my schooling in Budapest, and I faced ever-increasing antisemitism.

Labour Service

In March 1944, the German army occupied Hungary. The Hungarian people were not overly happy with the Germans being there, but Admiral Horthy, leader of the country, could not do anything about it. The country was militarily aligned with Germany and most of the Hungarian soldiers were fighting alongside the Germans in the Soviet Union. There was no opposition from the Hungarian army. It was a "friendly" occupation and some Hungarians, on seeing the soldiers, even cheered. I remember the German soldiers marching on the main street in immaculate uniforms; there were no tanks or cannons, only soldiers. It looked more like a parade than an occupation force.

Under German control, further restrictions were brought against the Jewish population. In April, Jews were ordered to wear a yellow Star of David on their outer clothes. I had been working an after-school job in a prestigious hat store, delivering hats to customers. In Hungary, the well-to-do did not carry their purchases. The manager liked me and gave me the deliveries where the tips were best. I made decent money, which helped our family because my father had been able to find only a menial job, which didn't pay very well, and we had a new addition to the family – my youngest brother, George, was born in 1943. Laci and Magda worked after school as well.

In the store there was another delivery boy, Pista, and we became friends. We helped each other with the deliveries. He wasn't Jewish, so he was able to get me things that I couldn't buy due to the new curfew hours in place for Jews. One day, I asked him if he would lend me his identity papers for a couple of hours so I could go shopping. He did so and nobody questioned me. Afterward, he offered to duplicate all of his papers, including his birth certificate. When I accepted, he told the priest of the village where he was born that he had lost his birth certificate, and asked to get another.

I used Pista's documents successfully for quite a while. Most of the time, I was not wearing the yellow star. I then suggested to my parents that I move out because it was so much easier to live under a false identity. If I lived on my own, I wouldn't be as exposed, and with these papers, I could buy them whatever they needed. My father thought it was a good idea, but that I should wait to see if things got worse before moving out. I was blond with blue eyes and most people did not think that I was Jewish. I was taking a lot of chances, thinking about what Gyula used to tell me about taking chances to get ahead in life. Once, to test myself, I went into the police station just to ask for directions, and they didn't question me or suspect I was Jewish.

Since 1939, Jewish males age twenty and older had been drafted into the army, to a specific unit for Jews called the labour service. Over the following years, different laws were created regarding the call-up age and the conditions under which Jews fought – by 1942, Jews were unarmed, treated miserably and forced to dig ditches and act as mine sweepers. I was fifteen years old when, in the beginning of May 1944, the army posted signs stating that all Jewish boys over fourteen years old must report to the army or face the penalty of severe punishment. Laci and I went to the reporting station, hoping for merely some indoctrination, but that didn't happen. We were told that from that minute on we were in the army and under military discipline; we were to work in the countryside because our brave soldiers were fighting in the Soviet Union. We were told that desertion was punishable by death and were instructed to report the next morning with one piece of luggage and await further orders.

At home, I told my parents that I should move out and live under the false papers, and not report to the army. My father knew an army officer and he asked him for advice. The officer said I would be sent to a farm close to the city to work, and would be safer there than I would be in the city. If I did not report, I could be shot. We decided that both Laci and I should report and that if problems arose, I could get the documents and go into hiding. I didn't take them with me for fear they would be found and taken away.

The next morning, when we went to the office, my brother was put in a different group. I, along with nineteen other boys, was taken to a large farm about thirty kilometres southeast of the city, near a town called Monor. We worked on the farm for sixteen hours a day, but the farmer and his family treated us well and we had lots to eat. We had to get up for work at 5:00 a.m., pausing for breakfast three hours later. At noon, when lunch was brought out, we rested for one hour and then worked until evening. After supper we washed up and did our laundry. We worked very hard, hoeing and weeding the fields, but we didn't mind because we felt we could stay there until the end of the war. There were hardly ever any visitors to the farm and we thought we were quite safe there.

We had no communication with anybody from home and we did not know that, starting in the middle of May, Hungarian gendarmes had been removing whole communities of Jews from the most eastern part of the country. I don't know if the Jewish population of Budapest had any knowledge of what was happening in the countryside, but we had no idea that all the Jews east of us had already been "resettled."

In the first week of July 1944, two Hungarian police officers armed with carbines came to the farm and took us to a nearby brickyard. The yard was fenced in and was full of Jewish people from the countryside. We found out that they were from all different villages in the area. There must have been at least 5,000 people there. Families with children and people of all ages huddled together with their luggage. I didn't think there was any room for us, but we were led to the loft of a shed by the fence. There were soldiers stationed all around the perimeter of the yard. I asked one standing close by, "Why are we here?" He replied that they were moving us to a different country to live. My group tried to speak to the officer in charge, telling him we were army soldiers sent here to work for the country, but he said he could not help because his orders were that all Jews, regardless of age, had to be transported out. He said he had a list of all the Jews living in the area that were to be resettled and, though we were not on it, one of the police officers remembered that there were Jews on the farm, which is why we were picked up as well. He claimed his orders were for all Jews to be shipped out and that he would get into trouble if he disobeyed. I tried to explain to the soldier beside the fence that if he let me get away my father would reward him. He said personally, if it were up to him, he would, but if he was found out, he would be shot.

I was thinking about how I could possibly get my false papers from home, but before I could even try anything, all the people from the brickyard, including us, were marched to the railway station and loaded into cattle cars. We were herded like cattle and I was separated from my friends. We were shoved and pushed. About sixty to eighty people were crowded into one boxcar and there was only a small, barred window for a little air and light. The smell and the heat from all the bodies was suffocating. There was not enough room to sit, so we were forced to stand. The cries of children made me feel terrible; I could do nothing.

No water or food was given to us. I didn't have any food with me, but some people were kind and gave me some; water, nobody seemed to have. It was dark and we didn't know where we were going. The day and night ran together and it grew quiet – only an occasional cry or call for help broke the silence. I think we were on the train for two full days and nights. The doors were not opened and there was no washroom. The smell was enough to get sick from. I was lucky because I happened to be under the little window and I could press my face to it for air. I did not know how long this nightmare would last. A few older people died, which created a little space, and some people sat on the bodies. It was an unbelievable hell. When we stopped and the doors were opened, we were in Poland, at Auschwitz.

Three Weeks

It was night and the place was lit up with floodlights. I saw German SS troops with machine guns and dogs. We were ordered out of the boxcars without our luggage. It was a cold but clear night and the scene surrounding me was unbelievable. SS soldiers were running with German shepherd dogs, yelling and occasionally shooting at people. The night was filled with thousands of people in total panic.

We were ordered to line up five abreast at the side of the boxcars. Some people in grey-and-blue striped clothing appeared. They looked like prisoners and began to remove the dead bodies and baggage from the boxcars. I stood in line by an open car door and one of these men asked me quietly if I spoke Yiddish. When I answered him, he whispered to that I should try to get out of here because our people were being killed. He said I should say I was eighteen years old. As the line moved forward, several people were shot because they stepped out of line or because they were trying to join the rest of their family, from whom they had been abruptly separated. The line slowly moved forward. I found myself in front of a table with two men behind it. One of them asked my name, my age and my occupation. I replied that I was eighteen years old and a farmer. He pointed to my right.

I looked around me and did not see a single person I knew. A panic took hold of me – here I was, alone, in a killing place, unable to do anything about it. I was crying to myself, Why was I here? What had

I done to deserve this? We were taken to a barracks, where we had to undress and line up in front of those same people dressed in striped clothing. I learned that they were Polish Jews. They cut off our hair and sprayed us with a white powder. Farther down the line, another man handed us clothing and shoes without any regard for size, and we each tried to exchange with others for better fitting clothes and shoes. Another gave us metal bowls. They also gave us each a number and told us that from then on we would be known only by this number. My number, 83631, was sewn onto my jacket. We were assigned to large barracks, a couple of hundred or so in each. There were kapos, overseers, assigned to each barracks, mostly Polish Jews who had been in the camp for a long time. I found out that some had become quite brutal in order to maintain these privileged positions.

Early in the morning, we had to line up to be counted. This lasted about two hours, and would soon become routine. It was a very long time to stand in one place. Some people fell down and were beaten. After being counted, we were given a piece of bread, about a one-inch square of margarine and a spoonful of jam; those were the daily rations. After that, there was nothing to do.

I noticed that the other side of our barracks housed groups of gypsies, and I started to talk to them. Some were Hungarians, others were Romanians. I was told that the place I was in was called Birkenau, and that it was surrounded with electrified wire fencing. One man told me that this place was a death camp and we were all going to be gassed and killed. I told him I didn't believe him, and he pointed to a large chimney with thick, black smoke coming from it. He said, "Look, there are your people burning today." I could not, I would not, believe that all those beautiful, innocent people, including children, were being murdered. I felt sick to my stomach and had to go to the toilet, which was like an outhouse, with no toilet paper at all. When I asked someone about the paper, they told me to find a smooth stone because there wasn't paper of any type available.

A couple of days went by. I saw some people run to the wire fence and touch it. They dropped dead; they had committed suicide. I could not help crying and feeling sorry for them and for myself. I felt miserable and alone in the world. I had been brought up Orthodox, but I crumpled in a corner, blaming God. We were supposed to be the chosen people. I asked God, For what had we been chosen – to die? I told myself that I did not believe that there was a God at all. God must just be a story. How could any God let all those humble, religious people die like that? I thought of the rabbi who had taught me, who was saintly and had always given most of his money to the poor. I accused God of allowing his people to be murdered. I fell asleep crying.

The next morning, I decided that I would try anything to get away from there. In the front of our barracks was a tiny room where the Polish Jewish kapo in charge slept. I approached him and, in Yiddish, asked him how to get out. The rest of the people in the barracks were Hungarians and spoke only Hungarian, so I don't think he minded speaking with me. He told me that almost every day there would be selections for work details, and that I should try and get on one.

That day, there was a selection and we had to line up. A German officer and a Jewish kapo were taking notes as they picked people from the line and made them stand to the side. I noticed that they picked only the strongest ones, which I was not. I was not selected. This went on for a few days, until one day I was selected with about thirty others and was taken to a different area. Here we had to open suitcases and divide and separate the contents into piles of clothing, food and other items. If we found any jewellery we were supposed to hand it over. Instead, we threw it into the latrine. From the contents, we could tell that the suitcases belonged to the Jews from Czechoslovakia, whose camp had been liquidated a few days earlier. Thousands had been sent to the gas chamber. I discovered food in some of the suitcases and for the first time in days, I ate real food. Going back to our camp, we were searched to see if we had stolen anything.

The next day I became sick with a cold, and I had a fever. There was no place to lie down except in the middle of the room, where there was a pail to use at night instead of going to the latrine, and a steel barrel with a fire in it for some heat. I lay there all night, with people stepping over me, but by the morning I felt somewhat better.

A week or so later we were ordered to stay in the barracks all day, with the warning that if we stepped out, we would be shot. We heard a lot of yelling and screaming and the sound of gunshots. We heard that the gypsies had been taken to the gas chambers. About 3,000 gypsies were murdered that day. By this time, we knew what that thick black smoke was. Nobody felt like talking. We were like locked-up animals, waiting for the unknown.

We had no news or even any rumours from the outside world. I had been in Auschwitz for about three weeks when we were lined up for selection for a work group to be taken somewhere else. This was the biggest group yet – about 2,000 people were selected. Again I was not chosen because I was small, but I took a chance as the group moved past me – I stepped out of my line and joined theirs. I was moved, along with the others, into an empty barracks. The next morning when we were lined up, I made sure that I was in the middle so as not to be easily seen. I was now in the transport that would take us out of this hellhole. We were marched to the same place where we had been brought a few weeks earlier. Once we were locked into the cattle cars again, the train pulled out of Auschwitz.

Taking Chances

We didn't know where the train was taking us, but anywhere had to be better than Auschwitz. We travelled for about three days. When the train finally stopped, we were let out into a camp beside a highway. We were assigned to single beds and given blankets, metal bowls and spoons. There was even a shower. We were told that we were in Mühldorf, Germany, and would be working in a forest. The camp was beside a main road and we saw a lot of traffic going by. I thought that we would be a little safer, being that close to the highway.

The next morning, we were given a loaf of bread to divide between four people, and jam and margarine. The camp commander gave a speech about this being a work camp. He said that if we worked hard we would be treated decently; if we tried to escape, we would be shot. "On the way to work," he said, "if you step out of line, you will be shot instantly by the guards." The whole area was surrounded by SS troops. We marched for about an hour before we reached the forest and were handed over to German civilian supervisors from the Organisation Todt. I learned that the project we were doing was called *Haupt Baustelle*, main construction site. We heard that there was another camp in the woods called the Waldlager, but I didn't meet anyone from there.

The Todt supervisors organized us into groups of different sizes. I was put together with twenty-nine other people and we were named the Tillman group because that was the name of our supervisor. He asked if anyone spoke German and I raised my hand. I had learned some in school, not very much, but because I could understand some Yiddish, I thought I might get away with it. He made me the group leader and told me to get three men and then…the last word sounded to me like "vercighorien." I understood that I was to take three men, but I didn't know the last word, so I said to the group, "He wants three of us to go with him. I do not know why." He took us to a shed and handed us axes, saws and other equipment.

Our job was to cut down huge trees. I noticed that almost everybody, thousands of people, were doing the same thing. We were in the middle of a dense, virgin forest where the trees must have been more than one hundred years old. We were given saws about five feet long with handles on each end and the foreman showed us how to use the saws and where to start the cut. It was very hard work and none of us were doing it too well. The foreman came over to me, grabbed the other end of the saw and started to work on the opposite side. In two minutes, I was exhausted. After showing us how he expected the work to progress he left, telling me to call him when we were halfway through cutting that tree. It took more than half of the day before I called him back. Then he took an axe and showed us how to wedge the opposing side of where we had cut to make the tree fall. Everywhere we looked, trees were falling.

My group had worked at that job for a few days when we lost our first person. When the trees were on the ground, tractors appeared, and the drivers tied chains to one end of the tree and pulled it away. There were tree stumps about two feet high everywhere. That day, when one of the long trunks was being pulled, it got stuck between two stumps, and as it was pulled forward it snapped back and hit one of our boys. He flew a few feet in the air and I think he died instantly. The drivers just threw him on a cart and took him away. Somebody started to say Kaddish. I did not even know the boy's name. We were all heartbroken and quiet, wondering who would be next.

Our foreman was unhappy with us and kept yelling that we were dirty, lazy Jews. The next morning he showed up with a new fore-man, who introduced himself as Herr Jacques from France, from the Alsace-Lorraine area. We were assigned to a different job, which in-volved cutting the branches of the fallen trees and pulling them away to a clearing. We were happy because the work was much easier and we could walk around instead of just staying in one place like before. Our new foreman was an elderly man and he was a decent person. He told me that as long we were doing something, he wouldn't bother us. He didn't yell or ask us to work faster. He liked to smoke his pipe, and left us alone.

After we had gathered a large amount of branches together, we were given a new task, making large bundles from the end pieces of the branches and tying them together. These were to be converted to wood gas and used as fuel for trains. Each bundle had to be small enough to be picked up by one person. It was not a difficult job, and we were soon building great walls from the bundles. We had to pro-duce around three hundred bundles a day. After a few weeks we had acres of bundles, but none were ever taken away. I knew it would be near impossible to count how many we were making each day, so when we had several rows fifty metres long and two metres high, we stopped and just pretended that we were working. Our foreman didn't care as long as he had his quota for the day. We kept on bring-ing bundles back when he wasn't looking, and we felt we were sabo-taging the war by not creating more fuel for their trains.

Herr Jacques told me he had been forced to take this job. He liked talking to me, and I was glad to listen because while he was talking I didn't have to work, and I was also learning the German language from him. He liked to talk politics, but my German wasn't good enough to understand everything, so I would simply respond, "Jah, so geht es" (yes, so it goes). This didn't bother him; he just continued talking. I think he was lonely. He often gave me his canteen and his lunch card and asked me to go get his lunch from the German kitchen, which was a fair distance from us. The Germans had an SS guard marching back and forth every one hundred metres around the outer edge of the forest. My foreman gave me a pass with which I was allowed to walk inside the work areas. Sometimes a foreman from a different group stopped me and asked why I was not working, but as soon as he recognized the pass, he let me continue. Occasionally the cook gave me a piece of bread, and on the way back I would stop at a latrine and fish out most of the meat from the canteen for myself. I figured that I needed it more than Jacques did. He would just comment, "I think the war will soon be finished because even we do not get much meat anymore."

The hunger in camp was overwhelming. We were so hungry that we would eat anything edible. The bread rations – an ersatz loaf of bread, which measured about thirty centimetres and looked like a brick – were reduced to share between five people and, later, six. We measured our sections per person by millimetres; every crumb was important. Some people tried to save a few bites for later, but I learned quickly that was not a good idea. Somehow, most of the time, it got stolen. The food was enough to keep us alive, but not for long. To work hard and not get proper nourishment was a sure recipe for dying. Apparently the Todt people also complained about not having adequate food.

Every few weeks, a new bunch of people were brought into our camp, but there were never more than 3,000 there at one time because so many continued to die, either from illnesses such as diarrhea, or at the workplace, from starvation and hard labour. A group of people were assigned to go around and pick up the dead or dying. The bodies were piled on a cart like firewood. Those people collecting the dead looked and acted like zombies. They didn't speak, didn't show any expression. No one cried or even seemed to care. There were no funerals; it was as if the dead was only a number, a total reduced by one. When the Nazis replaced our names with numbers, we became non-existent. It is much easier to kill a no-name than some-one who could be your namesake.

One day, when a new group was brought to our Lager, I recog-nized Mr. Katz, the baker from Újhely; he was the first person from home I had seen. He was in poor physical condition, so I told the supervisor that he was related to me, and he allowed me to take him into my group. Mr. Katz survived, and after the war he told me I had saved his life, that he felt half-dead when he arrived at the camp and could not have gone on for much longer.

The lack of food made us hungry all the time. Everybody was skin and bones. Starvation led most people to become single-minded about survival, and stealing or acting brutal to each other was com-mon. We felt dehumanized, our dignities taken away; our people stopped caring about anything or anyone. One night someone stole my shoes, which were under my bed, and left a much bigger pair in exchange. My feet were small and I had a hard time until I found somebody who wanted to exchange their pair with mine. The ones I received were still too large, and I had no choice but to put some pa-per from a cement bag inside them to reduce the space. It turned out that the paper worked as insulation and helped keep my toes from freezing.

Life in camp was routine. Line up early in the morning, receive our meagre daily rations, march through the gate and be counted. Work all day, line up to march back to camp, be counted again, line up to get soup. After all this, people were exhausted and most went to sleep.

Some of the Jewish kapos, the barracks' overseers, were so brutal that they were worse than some of the Germans. I think they were worried that if they weren't brutal they would lose their positions. There was a hierarchy – if you had some kind of position, you had a much better chance of survival. A cook could trade food for bet-ter clothing, a barber could trade for de-lousing powder, a doctor for medicine. Those who did not have connections were dying much sooner, and those who had been well-to-do at home were often the first to die. I think the poor were more used to being hungry and doing physical work, and were generally better at adjusting to camp life.

I was getting to be one of the longest residents in our camp. So many people had died or been taken away in selections that I hardly recognized anybody. The people in my group changed constantly – some were taken away and given different work, and others just did not show up in the morning. When a lot of new people were brought to the camp, a few were added to my group to replace those who had died. One of them, Weiner, spoke German perfectly and it didn't take him long to push me out of my position. Foreman Jacques spoke with him often, and a few days later when we got to our workplace, Weiner said that Herr Jacques had told him he was the new group leader and that I had to go to a different job. I could not believe Herr Jacques would do that. He had always seemed to trust me. I went looking for him and saw him with another foreman a little distance away. He waved me over, asking me what was wrong and why I wasn't working. When I told him about Weiner, he got very mad. He said, "I never made him the group leader; come with me." At our work station he called Weiner over and yelled at him. "You should have protected the young boy, not thrown him out!" He told Weiner to get out of his sight, that he didn't want to see him there again. I felt bad about it, but Weiner had been dishonest. Herr Jacques told me it was my fault and that I should not have let him push me aside. I told him I was only a kid and Weiner was an adult, and he agreed and repeated, "That is why I told him to get away from here. He should have protected you."

We worked for several months in the forest, until a large area was cleared away and the foundations for an underground factory were laid. We were told that an airplane factory would be built. While all of the other groups were involved in the extremely hard work of carrying heavy bags of cement all day long, my group stayed together and continued to cut and bundle branches. Herr Jacques still didn't care if we weren't working all the time. He saw that we had tons of bundles and that nobody wanted them. We adopted a system for warning when a German supervisor was going by – someone yelled the word, "Moko!" and others passed it down the line. This didn't mean anything in particular, but it was a code word to let everybody know a German was coming and that we should be working.

The weather was getting colder and we had no warm clothing. Without gloves, our fingers could not properly tie the wires on the bundles. I asked Herr Jacques if we could get a metal barrel to have a fire in, explaining that if we could not warm our fingers, we could not tie the bundles. He found a barrel, and we had enough wood to make a fire. He was the first to pull his chair close to the fire. He still counted the bundles every night, and I'm sure he noticed that we were bringing previously made bundles from the back of the rows. I made sure we had enough though, and he said he was pleased with the numbers.

As winter arrived our job with the bundles finished and our group was sent to work on cement construction. That was the worst job; people in the cement *Kommando* were dying quickly. When I got there, I was placed in a line to carry a bag of cement from a truck up a sloping board about thirty feet long, where a cement mixer worked non-stop. At the top, the bag was taken, and then the man went down to get in line again. When I got to the truck, two men put a bag of cement on my shoulder and I collapsed under the weight of it. I knew if I took the first bag up, I was a dead man. The supervisor ran over and started to beat me, but just then Herr Jacques came over and talked to him. The supervisor listened and told me to stand aside. Herr Jacques told me he had come looking for me and asked the other supervisor to give me an easier job because I was his translator. He was a good-hearted person, but that was the last time I saw him.

I was then given the job of removing the strings from the empty bags and rolling them into a ball. As I sat on the ground, the men above me kept throwing down the empty bags. The bags all had little bits of cement left in them and I was soon covered with cement powder. After work, when we were lining up to go back to camp, the project commander decided to reward the best worker. Because I was covered from head to toe with cement, he chose me and rewarded me with a package of cigarettes. I wasn't a smoker, but cigarettes were unavailable to Jews, so they were a valuable thing to have. There were people in camp so addicted that they were willing to give part of their bread rations for them. I gave one cigarette to the person who was distributing the evening food rations and I received a double portion of so-called soup. Nobody knew what kind of soup it was actually supposed to be – in it we tasted corn cobs, carrots, beans and some bones, but never meat. Every day, I got an extra portion for one cigarette. One small bite of food could mean an extra day of life.

Next the foreman gave me the job of standing on a wooden plank about six feet above the cement being poured into a giant mould, and I was to use a long pole to stir the cement to release the bubbles. An elderly man was doing the same thing as me. A German Todt employee was walking behind us and I witnessed him kick the elderly man's back. This man fell into the still-soft cement and the German would not allow anyone to help him get out. He was buried alive.

The following morning, I decided to hide in camp and not go to work. As we were marching toward the front gate, I snuck out of line and hid on top of the latrine. We were usually counted as we were going through the front gate, so I figured that I would not be missed because I would not be counted as leaving. During the day, I hid and occasionally managed to beg some food from the kitchen. The kitchen area was behind a wire fence, but the cooks threw some food over it for me. I hid like this for a few days until one time, as I was in line looking for a chance to sneak out, one of the German soldiers who was walking beside us, without looking at me, whispered, "Today, go to work." Surprised, I did. When we returned from work that evening, I found out that everybody who had been hiding in camp had been taken away to be murdered. I don't know why that soldier saved me; I did not know him. Maybe it was because I was with the first group when the camp opened, and he had seen me often, or maybe because I was blond with blue eyes. I guess I will never know.

While I was hiding in the camp, I saw a couple of one-engine planes land in the nearby field. I thought that if I could find someone who could fly a plane, it would be worth trying to escape. I knew that it was possible to sneak through the guards at the work site, but then what? We were in a forest and wouldn't know which way to go; we didn't speak proper German; and we had no money, no clothes and no contacts. It was hopeless. I never heard of any successful escapes from the camp.

One morning, an announcement was made: no one would be going to work and we were to clean the camp instead. We were given soap to wash with and better food than ever before. There were whispers about a Red Cross inspection. The following morning, at the lineup, there was a selection. Along with the weaker people, I was selected. I thought, this is the end, they are taking us to our deaths and we can't do anything about it.

The Forest Camp

To my surprise, we were led to the Waldlager, the forest camp about two hours walking distance away. This camp was completely different from the one I had been in. There were hardly any buildings – most of the shelters were underground bunker-type spaces. Only a small chimney on a mound of earth, which formed the roof, was visible. The camp took up a large area but was smaller than the main camp, and to me it looked older and rougher.

We waited in line for someone to tell us where to go. A tall man came over to our group, looked us over and asked me to follow him. He took me to a bunker that he was in charge of. He was a French prisoner and had picked me because I was the youngest of the group and, though he did not like Hungarians, he had to get someone because one of his men had died. This turned out to be my luckiest day since I had left home because the people in this bunker were the elite of the whole camp. They spoke mainly French among themselves, so I'm not sure if any of them were Jewish. The people in the camp were from all over Europe and besides some Jews, there were Russian prisoners of war and political prisoners. I learned that most of the cooks were Greek Jews from Saloniki. In my previous camp, the inmates had been only Hungarian and Polish.

Michel was the name of the leader who had chosen me. I think he was an officer in the French army, and most others seemed to be in the military as well, judging by the way they took orders from Michel.

Most of these people were working in the camp – one was a doctor, another was a cook, one worked with clothing and another was a barber. Even the Germans did not bother them.

Michel took me under his protection and managed to get me work cleaning the roads, getting firewood for the pot-bellied stove, and anything else that needed to be done inside the camp. I was given better-fitting, warmer clothing, had my hair cut and got more and better food from the kitchen. Maybe it was due to the better food, or the amount of it, that I got ill and had diarrhea. I knew that in the camp, it was a deadly sickness. I told Michel, who spoke to the doctor. He said he didn't have any medication but that I should eat a piece of charcoal. One of our people worked at charcoal-making and brought me a piece. I took a bite, but my mouth went completely dry and I couldn't swallow it. The doctor told me that if I didn't eat it, I would die. After he and the cook discussed something in French, the cook brought me a piece of soft and smelly cheese and put small pieces of coal inside, and I managed to swallow several pieces. It worked and I got better.

It was during this period that I learned there was a small medical facility in camp, but every third day, all the patients were taken away and nobody ever saw them again. The Jewish doctors made sure that those who could walk got out before they were taken out. It grew difficult to keep me inside the camp, so Michel let me know that he had decided to send me out with the charcoal-making group, who would somehow look after me.

At the charcoal workplace I learned how to place logs in a circle, with their tips joining, leaving space in the middle for a fire. We then covered the outside of the wood with earth and lit a fire inside. The fire burned slowly because it did not get much air, and the logs slowly turned into charcoal. I had not been assigned to the group, so every time a German came by a signal was given ahead of his approach and I was hidden in a large tool box, covered by an old blanket and tools. Luckily, this did not happen often.

During work time, my duty was to bake the potatoes the field workers had stolen. I put the potatoes in the hot earth on top of the slowly burning logs, and they cooked in about one hour. We charged the field workers one potato for every three that we baked. The baked potato became our means of trade, and everybody in our bunker divided whatever payment we received for them.

One day, one of the inmates from my previous camp came by and told me we were just about the last survivors from the original 3,000 who had come from Auschwitz. He told me that after I had left, three people managed to get away but were recaptured after two days. The Germans assembled the prisoners and hanged the escapees as a warning to the others.

We heard that the underground airplane factory was progressing well, which worried us. After the forest had been cleared, the soil was used to make a 200-metre long and 20-metre high shape that was then covered with about three metres of solid, reinforced concrete; after the earth was removed, a huge cement hangar remained. We doubted any bomb could penetrate it. We all hoped that the war would be over before that factory was finished.

~

In the middle of March 1945, there was an Allied air attack on the city of Mühldorf. Planes flew over our camp and we heard bombs exploding. Someone explained to me that it was a precision bombing, which meant that the planes were attempting to hit a specific target. The attack went on for a while and there wasn't even one German defense plane in the sky. Afterward, a lot of us were brought to the outskirts of the city to clean up all the debris.

This was the first time we were near the city of Mühldorf. We were not more than ten kilometres away. We were divided into groups and I was with about twenty others who were led to the railway station, where several trains were burning. We saw smoke everywhere. Our group was supposed to empty a boxcar full of sugar. We were given bags to fill with sugar, and they were loaded onto trucks and driven away. One German soldier stood guard with his rifle on his shoulder, and one of our men got behind him and hit him on the head with a metal bar, killing him. Some of the boys picked up the body and hid it under the overturned boxcar. Nobody noticed it while we were there, and we got back to camp without any problems. This incident made us feel that the end of the war was approaching.

Soon after this, Michel, the leader of the French prisoners, managed to get in touch with the French underground through one of the supervisors who was also from Alsace-Lorraine. We were told that the war was going well and the Americans were getting closer. That news really built up our morale. Getting news from the outside world in itself brought us hope that we might get out of this miserable place.

The contact with the French underground changed the situation in our group. Discussions turned to heated arguments. I knew that I was often the subject of these talks because they referred to me as the "plus petit," which I guessed meant the littlest one. From Michel, I learned that they were planning an escape and that I'd be included. He admitted that there was a lot of opposition to this, but in the end they all agreed.

We had been receiving civilian clothing one piece at a time and hiding it until eventually we all had enough. The plan was that as the Americans got closer, the underground would create a disturbance at one side of the camp. When all the attention was focused there, we'd escape on the opposite side, where the underground would be waiting for us and would quickly take us to a safe place. We hadn't finalized our plans when, near the end of April, we were informed that the Germans were planning to evacuate the camp.

Our plans had to change. We informed our contact that we would try to get out of line as we walked through the woods. Michel assigned people numbers for the order in which we were to leave. I was given number thirteen. Michel chose to be the last one to go. We had been assured that the French underground would be waiting for us. In the forest, everything went according to plan – one at a time, the first eight managed to get out of the line and disappear into the woods. We noticed that the German guards were not paying as much attention as they had in the past. However, we arrived at the railway station before the rest of the group had a chance to escape.

An empty train of cattle cars stood waiting for us. Our group managed to stay together. Michel and some of the other men had screwdrivers and other tools hidden on them and as soon as we were locked in, we tried to break through the sliding door on the opposite side. The train pulled out, but we knew that the French underground would follow it. We travelled for a couple of hours, then stopped for a long time and heard other trains going by. Our train started moving again, but shortly after, we were pushed off to a side track. Through the small window we saw trains going by, full of soldiers. After a while our train was pushed back to the main track and we moved in a direction and destination unknown to us. We would move, stop and then move again for short periods of time. Finally, the train came to a full stop. By this time it was getting dark, and we had successfully managed to take the hinges off the door and slide it slightly open. Michel thought it was not dark enough to start our escape, so we waited. Finally, he told number nine to go. The man jumped off, ran down a small slope and across an empty field to the forest and disappeared. Then number ten took off, and so on.

When I was told to go, with great anticipation I jumped off and started to run down the slope. I wasn't all that far away when Michel yelled for me to come back. Apparently one of the German guards had unlocked the door and seen that the door on the other side was open. He raised his gun and tried to get to the door we had escaped from to shoot. Somebody knocked him down while at the same time many hands were trying to help him up, and he got tangled in it all. By this time I had gotten back and several hands reached out and pulled me in. A lot of our people were around the soldier, creating confusion. He was yelling, "I am going to shoot all of you!" Michel spoke up, telling him nobody had escaped and that we just needed fresh air. The soldier ordered everybody to one side and started to count us. Those who had been counted had to move to the other side of the car. It was quite dark, and those who were already counted crawled back, confusing him completely. Then Michel told him that he better not say anything at all about the incident because he'd be charged and killed by the SS.

The soldier made us close the broken door and he sat down by the other door with his feet hanging down. Michel whispered to me, "Do not worry, we will continue later." It grew quiet and I fell asleep. I woke up to yells that the war was over and that we were all free. The door was open and there were no German soldiers anywhere. It was early in the morning and a slight mist was over the fields. I jumped out from the boxcar, as did other people, and we all began running across an empty field to a village about four hundred metres away. We hadn't eaten since leaving the camp. I'm sure we were all thinking about getting food in the village.

The first houses in the village were behind some bushes. I had almost reached these bushes when I saw German SS soldiers hiding behind them. I got down on my stomach and tried to crawl back to the train. The Germans started to fire, shooting at us indiscriminately. There was nowhere else to go; the field was surrounded. I saw people falling and was afraid to even lift my head. I managed to reach the train platform. I stood up and started off to find the car I had been in, the one with the broken door. I was running by an open door when a man yelled, "Get in or you're going to get killed!" He reached out, grabbed my hand and was pulling me in when a shot was fired. I was on my stomach, halfway in the car, when the bullet hit the man who was pulling me. He fell out just as I got in. Somebody quickly pushed the door shut. Only a few people were in this car. I broke down crying and the others joined in, crying for those who had been tricked and murdered.

We heard gunfire for a while longer, then quiet. We stayed in the car, not daring to open the door and look out. We heard yelling in

German and footsteps running by our door. Suddenly, the train jerk-
ed and started to move. Nobody opened our door. One of the men
looked through the little window and told us it was daytime. I glanced
around and saw that only fifteen of us were in this boxcar. I was wondering if the other cars had been equally reduced because if they had,
it was possible that hundreds had been killed on that field. The train
continued for a couple of hours, then stopped again. We stayed in one
place all day and night. By this time we were so weak and thirsty that
we didn't care what was happening to us anymore.

Later the next morning the doors were opened and we found ourselves looking out onto a large village with houses right up to the railway station. Villagers brought a wagon with a huge kettle full of soup
and we were ordered out to form a line. Now, I could see that several
hundred of us were missing, no doubt killed on that field. I could not
see Michel or any of the others from my group. I had just reached the
wagon and gotten a little soup in a bowl when planes appeared and
started shooting at us. One of the first bullets hit the person on the
wagon serving the soup. I jumped into the ditch beside the tracks,
remembering what I had been taught in Hungary, that when a plane
shoots, you should lie facing towards it in a ditch. One bullet hit the
leg of the man lying beside me and it tore off all the flesh of his leg,
just the bone was left. He was bleeding and crying, and I could not do
anything to help him.

When the planes had passed I jumped up, ran to the wagon and
dipped my bowl in the kettle for another helping of soup. The planes
made a second pass overhead but this time they were dropping
bombs on the tracks in front and behind the train. They were American planes and had probably realized that we were not German soldiers. The Germans, furious, began beating us to force us back into
the boxcars. One of them hit me on the head with his gun but luckily for me, he lost his footing and only the tip of his gun touched my
head. I got into one of the cars, my head bleeding badly. Somebody
tore off a part of my shirt and tied my head with it. Eventually the

bleeding stopped, but with all the blood on me and my shirt it looked like I was seriously hurt.

The train could not move because of the bombed tracks and we were stuck in front of the village. We were locked in the boxcar again that night. At daybreak, the doors of the train were opened by three German soldiers who laid down their guns and said that the Americans were just outside the village. They told us they had stayed behind to open the doors for us, saying, "We are just soldiers, not SS, and did not do anything wrong. The SS guards have all run away." I was suspicious and kept wondering if it was the same trick as before, but this time, it was not. It was April 30, 1945, and we had been liberated at the village of Seeshaupt.

I walked toward the first house I saw with two other men who stayed with me because they knew I could speak a bit of German. I asked the middle-aged woman who opened the door if she had anything to eat and she invited us in. The three of us sat at her table and she gave us each a glass of milk and told us she would make us breakfast. She opened her cupboard and took out all the eggs she had, as well as some meat, which I think was ham. We had not eaten a proper breakfast for almost a year. We ate everything she prepared and asked for more but she showed us that nothing was left. We walked up the street, knocked on other doors and were given more food.

Continuing farther along, we arrived at the main street. Just then, I saw the first American tank column. As we were standing by the roadside, the American soldiers threw chocolate bars to us. The tank columns went through the village nonstop, followed by trucks full of soldiers. The trucks stopped and these soldiers stayed in the village. By this time I was not hungry, and I started to look for a doctor for my head injury. I spoke to a soldier with a red cross on his helmet, but he couldn't speak German. I pointed to my head and he led me to a medical tent where a doctor worked on me. After, he called over a soldier who spoke German, who told me that I should have had stitches, but that now it was too late. So I was to have a large gash on the top of my head, a souvenir from this war.

The soldier asked me to follow him, and we were joined by another man who was also being treated there. I think his name was Joseph and he was a Polish Jew from our camp. We followed the soldier to another unit and were handed over to a group of ten soldiers assigned to help the Jewish survivors. By this time, it was noon and the soldiers were getting their lunch. The soldier who had been looking after me brought his lunch over to me. I ate it, then the next soldier also brought his lunch to me, and then the remaining soldiers all put their lunches in front of us. We divided the food and put it in our pockets for later. I knew I shouldn't have done this, but I couldn't help feeling insecure. I wasn't hungry then, but I was thinking, will I have food later?

The soldiers conferred and after a while motioned us to follow them. We couldn't understand English, but one of them spoke a little German and we managed to figure out what they wanted us to do. We followed them into the middle of the village and stopped at a beautiful house. A large, matronly woman opened the door. Inside, sitting in the living room, was a very well-dressed woman. She was the owner of the house and told us that her husband was the mayor and that he was a general in the army. The women did not know whether he was still alive. The soldiers ordered them to move out of the house and into the coach house that was on the property.

We went to a bedroom and looked in the closet, which was full of men's clothing. The mayor must have been short because some of his clothes fit me loosely, though better than what I had on. I found the washroom and took a bath for the first time in almost a year, and then I got clean underwear and selected some sporty-looking clothes. I felt reborn, until I looked in the mirror and could not recognize myself. I was skin and bones. With my bandaged head I looked so awful that I started to cry, feeling sorry for myself. The person who looked back at me in the mirror was a scared-looking skinny little boy, not the person I thought I was. I do not think I weighed more than one hundred pounds.

Like a Dream

The soldiers from the American army kitchen brought us supper, then came back to the house after we had finished eating. They had found a large wine cellar with a good quantity of wine still in it. They started to drink and sing, and made me drink with them. I remember getting sick and going into the washroom, vomiting. I don't remember who put me to bed. Many of the newly liberated prisoners died due to eating too much, so it was actually lucky that I got drunk and threw up.

When I woke up, Joseph was in the bed with me. He told me that he had put me to bed because I was sick to my stomach and had passed out. He also said that more soldiers had arrived the night before and almost everybody had gotten drunk and made a mess of the place. I asked the women in the coach house to clean up the place. They weren't too pleased, but it was their house so, reluctantly, they did clean up. One pleaded with me that we not destroy the place because she had nothing else left but this house.

We had nothing to do all day, so I walked on the streets and talked to people. They all claimed they didn't know about the massacre of the Jewish populations of Europe. They tried to be friendly, but I just couldn't accept any of their invitations to come into their houses. I asked if there were any Jews left in the village. They looked embarrassed when they answered no. When I asked how many Jewish people lived in the village before the war, they said they did not remember any. I didn't believe them.

A few days later, we were moved to a collection compound in Munich, which was about fifty kilometres away. We were free to do anything we wanted; it was mainly a place to try to rehabilitate us to normal life. The American Jewish Joint Distribution Committee (JDC) provided us with civilian clothing and three regular meals a day, and in the evening there was entertainment. In a theatre, listening to music and watching all the people enjoying the entertainment, it felt like what had happened was a bad dream. A few days ago we were dying from hunger and thirst, and now we were singing and dancing.

During my first day in Munich, a man was badly beaten by some other survivors. When I asked why, they told me he was a kapo and had been very cruel. I said, "Was he not another Jew?" Later, I asked that man why he had mistreated other Jews. He started to cry and told me the Nazis had trained him like you train a dog. He had been ordered to be a kapo, and the first time he was told to beat a person, he refused and was beaten instead. The next time, he hesitated and was again beaten. The third time, he beat the man a little and was given an extra portion of food. The next time, it was easier to beat someone. He was rewarded and given special privileges. From that time on, he did not think, just did what he was asked to do. He told me he was so sorry and that he was not that type of person before the war. He was Polish and had been in the camps for four years. I didn't know whether to feel sorry for him or hate him for what he had done to his own people.

I went out for a walk. I was walking down a wide street where most of the houses were bombed out and in some only the walls were still standing. The streets were mainly deserted. A very good-looking young blond girl was walking toward me. She stopped and asked me if I had any American cigarettes. I nodded; we had been given cigarettes. She said, "If you give me five cigarettes, I will make love to you." She told me there were no men left in her family and that she was trying to support her mother and her little brother. I hesitated, but she took my hand and led me into an empty building. A few minutes later, we came out and I gave her my whole pack of cigarettes. It wasn't as big a deal as I had anticipated, but it did give me a mental uplift. All of a sudden, I was not just a number. It's hard to explain, but because this beautiful German girl wanted to make love to me (never mind the cigarettes) after the Nazis had made us feel that we were nobodies, I was a human being again. In that few minutes, I regained my dignity and self-esteem. I was not a number anymore.

I turned around, went back to the office of our compound and asked for help to get back to Hungary. I was eager to find out what had happened to my family. I think that before that, subconsciously, I had been trying to avoid reality. I was sure that nobody had survived and I was left alone. I didn't know what I'd do with my life if I didn't find anyone from my family alive. I had nothing – no education, no country, no money. My future did not look promising.

I stayed in Munich for a few more days and explored the city with a group of other Hungarians. We saw a long line in front of a store and, walking over, saw it was a bakery. People were lining up to get bread. One of us suggested that we try to get some freshly baked bread. We walked to the front of the line and without a word, people parted and let us in. We didn't have any money. My companions pushed me to the front and told me to just ask for bread, so I did. Without a word, I was handed a loaf. Each one of us got a loaf and walked out. Nobody asked us for money. We felt they owed it to us and perhaps they felt the same.

We were soon moved to Feldafing, to a former Hitlerjugend training camp, where the American army had a base. It was a beautiful place in the mountains. The army occupied most of the facility and supplied us with food, organizing everything. The food and the care we were given helped us regain some of our health. One day, an American soldier asked me if I wanted to go with him to practise shooting. Naturally, I did. We went to a field, set up some empty tin cans and began shooting at them. All of a sudden, some Germans hiding in the mountains opened fire on us, using machine guns with tracer bullets. One bullet missed my head by inches. We got down on our stomachs and crawled back to safety. We reported the incident, but nobody wanted to fight anymore so they just ignored the whole thing. I really did not blame them; the war was over.

A few weeks had passed since my liberation and I was restless. I felt stronger and wanted to get away from Germany. Nonetheless, I was already determined not to live in Hungary anymore either. I went into the office and again asked for help to get out. I told them I wanted to go back to Hungary to find out if any of my family had survived. The people there were sympathetic and agreed to try to help me. I was told I'd have to go back to Munich because only from there were transports being organized to different countries.

I was taken back to Munich, alone. The others wanted to stay longer in Feldafing. I was back in the same place I'd been before, making the same request. I was told that the Hungarians were not yet being organized for a return. At present, transports were being organized to Czechoslovakia. The next day I returned, claiming to be a Czechoslovakian from Slovenské Nové Mesto, the border city near Hungary where my father had once owned a tavern.

A short time later, around the middle of June, I was accepted on a transport being organized to go to Czechoslovakia through Hungary. In the group I met a girl about my age who wanted to go to Košice to see if any of her family had survived. She told me her name was Olga and asked me if we could travel together. I was glad because I also felt very lonely.

At the Hungarian border, we got off the train and walked across a field to the Hungarian railway station. The train to Budapest was already so full that people were standing on the steps. I didn't know how we were going to get on that train. But just then two Russian soldiers walked by, picked me up and tossed me through the open window, where I fell on top of people, followed by my new friend, who landed on top of me. We got to our feet, to the angry shouts of the people we had knocked over. When they saw that we were two young kids, they made room for us. That was when we learned that the Soviets had occupied Hungary.

I would not say it was a comfortable trip, but compared to the boxcars it was luxurious. The train moved slowly, and it was morning by the time we got to Budapest. I promised Olga that I would come back to the station to tell her what or who I found. Our plan was that if we didn't find any of our family members, we would go together to Palestine. Some survivors had decided to go straight to Palestine; in Munich, I had met a representative from the Jewish Agency who urged us to go there.

I didn't have money for the streetcar, so I walked to our apartment. My heart was beating fast when I knocked on the front door where we used to live. The door opened and there was my father, looking at me. He did not speak, just grabbed me and held me to his chest. I think he was crying and didn't want me to see. I couldn't talk either, and just started to cry. My father was alone in the house. He told me that my sister, Magda, was alive but not home right then – she had been in hiding with gentile friends. My mother was suffering from depression and had gone with Fredi and my little brother George to her mother's house in Bótrágy, Czechoslovakia. My mother's brother, my uncle Moritz, had survived and was also there. His wife and three children had died in Auschwitz. He and my mother were the only survivors of their large family.

Then my father told me that my older brother, Laci, had died in the last few days of the war. He had been liberated somewhere near Budapest by Soviet troops, but as he and ten of his group started to walk to Budapest, they were recaptured by retreating Germans. All of them were shot. One of the boys was only wounded, and a farmer found him and saved him. He was the one who had brought the news of how the others had died.

I told my father I had to go to the railway station because my friend was expecting me back, and we got on my father's bicycle, me sitting on the front bar. I saw Olga waiting in front of the station. I introduced my father to Olga and told her that I was staying in Budapest. She was crying with happiness that I had reunited with family, but I felt she was also crying at being alone again. We wished her luck with finding some of her own family and we returned home.

My father and I spent most of the night talking. He told me how Raoul Wallenberg, the Swedish diplomat, had saved him. My father hadn't been drafted into the Hungarian labour service until later in 1944, due to his connections. At some point, he was given a two-day pass from his work for the army. When he got back to the city, members of the Hungarian fascist Arrow Cross Party captured him and forced him to go, with others, to a brickyard where a group was about to be sent to a labour camp, on what was later to be called a death march. As they were about to leave, Wallenberg pulled up in his limo and demanded they let those who had the protective Swedish *Schutzpass* go free. My father didn't have a pass, but he stepped forward and said that he did, but had left it at home. Mr. Wallenberg said, "I remember you, get in the line," and he personally escorted them back to the city. My father told me that Wallenberg was not Jewish, yet he was saving Jews. People could not believe the chutzpah that man had. He even confronted the notorious Eichmann, the main authority in charge of deporting all the Hungarian Jews.

I wanted to know more about my family and asked my father to tell me what he knew of the fates of all my cousins and uncles. He told me that everybody, as far as he knew, had died in Auschwitz. But we still had hope that someone would show up, as I had.

The next day, I took the train to my grandmother's house to see my mother and my brothers. The whole area was occupied by the Russians; there were no borders. I got off at the village station and noticed that nobody else was there – I was the only person getting off the train. I started to walk and finally saw a farmer going by with a horse and buggy. I asked him if he would mind taking me to my grandmother's house, to the Weiszs'. He replied, "Your grandmother Mrs. Weisz was mother for the whole village. She was always ready to help anybody, but she was taken away and never came back."

When I got off the buggy, my mother was sitting outside in the front yard. She looked up and thought she was hallucinating; it took her a while to believe that it was really me. After she regained her composure she said she had never given up hope for my survival. It was like a dream for me. My father, mother, sister and younger brothers were alive. And my uncle's survival gave me hope that maybe more of our family had survived. Unfortunately, no one else from our family returned.

We spent a few days talking and telling each other what had happened since the last time we were together. I could not let her hand out of mine, just to make sure that it was not a dream. I learned that her courage and resourcefulness had saved the rest of our family. She told me that once, Nazi soldiers came to their apartment building and ordered everybody downstairs. My mother put a sign on their door that said infectious patients were staying there, and though all the other people were taken away, the soldiers did not open their door – they must have been afraid of being infected.

My mother and brothers soon went back to Budapest, while I stayed with my uncle for a few more days to finish the harvest so we would have some food to take back to Budapest. My uncle owned the only threshing machine in the village. The farmers paid for threshing partly with money and partly with food. Although food was difficult to find in the city, in the countryside, it was easy to buy if you had money.

At the end of June 1945, we heard that the Soviets were re-establishing and closing the borders out of Bótrágy. Areas that had previously been part of Czechoslovakia now became Carpatho-Rus, a part of Ukraine that had been ceded to the Soviets. My uncle said we'd have to leave everything and that we wouldn't be coming back. We gathered as much food as we could carry and immediately took the train to the border, but we were too late. There were Russian soldiers all over the place, checking documents. Everybody on the train had to have documents allowing them to leave the country.

We got off the train and started to walk back to the nearest village. My uncle asked some locals in a restaurant what to do, and they suggested we walk past the railway station until we reached a sharp bend in the tracks where the train had to slow down. There, we could jump on the train. We found the place and waited in the ditch, along with others. As the train slowed, some people jumped on, but a Russian soldier was standing on the step of the first car and saw them. As the soldier followed them onto the cars they had gotten on, my uncle yelled, "Now!" We jumped on the train and I lay down on a seat, pretending to be asleep. My uncle could speak Russian, and he pretended to be reading a Russian newspaper he had. One of the soldiers came in, looked at us and then passed us right by.

On the train, my uncle told me his story of survival. When he first heard that Jews were being deported, he left the village where everybody knew him and got a job in another village where no one knew he was Jewish. He was a big man, used to farm work. He worked the fields with another man and was still there when the Soviet army liberated the village. For no reason, they picked him and a few other stronger men and shipped them to Siberia to work, as they were doing to many men after the war. My uncle claimed that he was a cook, figuring that a cook always had food. He spent a month in Siberia. After a while, he managed to prove that he was a Jewish survivor and was released.

When we got back to Budapest, it was the first time all of our surviving family members were together. My little brother George was only a year old when I left; now he was walking. And my brother Fredi was entering Grade 7. I had a joyful reunion with my sister, Magda, who was back from the countryside, where she had been visiting the people who had hidden her during the war.

With the amount of food we brought back, my mother made dinner the way she used to before the Germans came into our life. Magda told me how she had survived as a Catholic during the war. One of her friends took her to her parents' house in a small village and introduced her to everyone, including the local priest, as a cousin from Budapest. She wore a cross on a chain around her neck, and on Sundays she went to church with the family. Occasionally, she managed to go back to Budapest and bring some food for the rest of our family. When she visited, she told them there were no Jews left in that village and nobody there thought that any Jews were left in the country. They pretended as though Jews had never existed in the village, and she did not bring the subject up for discussion.

In time, my father opened a textile store on a main street in the city, sharing the space with a hat store. He was doing well and I was able to continue with my schooling, but I told my parents it was only temporary and that I didn't want to live in Hungary.

I hadn't been home more than two months when one Sunday my father decided we should all go to a beach just east of the city. It was a nice sandy beach by the Danube River and I waded in up to my chest, trying to learn to swim. I took a couple of strokes and was about to stand up but I had drifted and suddenly there was no earth under my feet. I was out in the fast-flowing river. I yelled for help and went under. I surfaced, yelling again, noticing people standing by the shore looking, but there wasn't anyone else in the water. I went under again, in my mind already thinking, what would my mother do if I drowned? Coming up again, somehow I got hold of something; it was an oar and I grabbed it, overturning a kayak. I climbed on the kayak and helped the man who had just saved me to hold on to it until a motorboat pulled us to shore. I got violently sick from swallowing so much water. When I felt somewhat better, I couldn't find the man who had saved me. I hadn't had a chance to thank him. I was almost a kilometre downriver, and it took me a while to walk back to my family. My mother asked, "Where were you? Did you hear a boy was drowning in the river?" I said no, I was just out walking. She never found out that it was me.

That summer, I got a job in a dental laboratory and grew interested in dentistry. In the fall of 1945, I started dental school and worked in the laboratory in the afternoons. It was a program where, upon graduation, you could do most dental procedures but you did not receive a degree. After a couple of years, I quit the afternoon job and with the experience I had, got a position as a dental technician at Szilas and Cain, the best laboratory in the city. I was getting paid considerably more than I had been getting before. Mr. Szilas was the president of the laboratories association and Mr. Cain was a secretary of the dental union. They were very good to me and taught me way beyond the required curriculum. At their dental offices, they both treated patients in the evenings, and I assisted them whenever I had an opportunity.

In March 1948, at the end of the second school year, I was elected president of the student union representatives to the faculty. I think that led to me also being elected to organize the 100-year anniversary parade of Hungary's freedom from the Habsburgs' rule. Each school was to join the parade at a different time and place, and I had to work out these details. The task was challenging because every trade and profession had to participate, and close to half a million people were expected to march. After my part of the organization was all set, I had to represent the youth of the country by holding the national flag behind the country's leader, Mátyás Rákosi. I wasn't pleased about this, but I couldn't think of any way to refuse this honour. I kept hiding my face behind the flag, concerned about being recognized, since I was planning on leaving the country.

Searching for Normal

During the days, I was functioning like a normal person of my age. At night, it was a different story. I was lying in a comfortable bed, but I couldn't sleep. The faces of the dying and the dead kept coming back. I was seeing the faces of some of the Orthodox people in camp; how, in that misery, were they still believers? While living in desperate conditions they were praying and reciting Kaddish each time somebody died. I admired their faith in God.

I kept asking myself why I was alive when so many people around me had died, and I constantly thought about all the people who had been good to me. How had I continued to live even when I was supposed to die? I didn't know anyone who had survived in the camps after being as sick as I was. I thought about my brother Laci, who was a gentle soul, who would not have even killed a bug, and how he had died on a field, unknown. I also thought about Olga, a young girl alone in the world. I felt somewhat guilty for letting her go so easily when I reunited with my father. I hope that she found somebody from her family alive. I thought about all the mundane things I was involved in during the day. How we take such unimportant things in life so seriously. I was young in age but I felt old, and I usually fell asleep crying.

In the morning I put on my normal teenaged face and participated in activities. I joined the Labour Zionist organization and became best friends with four other boys my age – Misi, Bandi, Szusz and Pista. People called us the five twins because if only some of us were invited to an affair, none of us would go. We spent time learning about Zionism, singing Hebrew songs and going to dances. We had fun times and had girlfriends. I thought I was in love with a girl named Adriane, a nice girl who had joined our Habonim labour Zionist group. Everything was going well until she invited me to go to the theatre with her one Saturday. I went to meet her at her home, a fancy building downtown. Her father told me that we were all going to the opera. We got in their car, with their professional driver. I didn't like the opera or the parental supervised dating, and I broke up with her shortly after.

During summer holidays, I went to a Zionist camp in the Carpathian Mountains, where we received training in judo and fighting by Israeli trainers called *shlichim*, emissaries, who were preparing us for our eventual move to Palestine. One day I borrowed a bicycle and rode along the mountainous paths to visit my younger brother Fredi, who was in a more Orthodox Zionist camp by the water. As I was riding downhill, my bicycle hit a stone and I flew about five metres into the air, landing on a pile of stones that had been left there by a road construction crew. Instinctively, I put my left hand down, and with my right hand I somersaulted off the pile of stones. I arrived at Fredi's camp bleeding from both hands and created quite a bit of excitement, but my training saved me from serious injury. My brother was playing Ping-Pong when he heard of my bloody entry and came running. I assured him my wounds were not serious, just scrapes, and my hands were soon bandaged at the camp's infirmary. I had a nice visit, and even participated in shooting practice. Many water snakes slithered around the shoreline, which made the campers afraid to get into the water. The snakes came up to the surface to get air, and from shore I shot nine out of ten, which was the camp record. It made my brother feel better about my less than glorious entrance.

Back in the city, I had to attend a national annual dental union meeting. Mr. Cain, the secretary, had insisted I attend. I talked my friends into coming to keep me company; they weren't members but they managed to get in with me. I noticed that Mr. Cain was running the meeting. To bring some excitement to a dull time, I got up and questioned why the president wasn't there for a national annual meeting. I stated that members had come from all parts of the country and the president should welcome their participation. There was general agreement, and a decision was made to elect a new president. As a joke my friends started to yell, "We want Miklos for president!" I told them to be quiet but they wouldn't listen and kept yelling in unison and making a lot of noise. Mr. Cain, to bring order, agreed to have an election for a new president and appointed a nominating committee. I was one of the three candidates chosen. He called for voting and I think because of the loud yelling of my name, I won the most votes and became the president of the dental union! I could not stop my friends from laughing and insisting on saying to me, "Yes Mr. President, no Mr. President, we'll do what you command, Mr. President." It took quite a bit of time for them to stop heckling me.

I took the job seriously. The union owned a big building in the best part of the city. With the union's money I established a library and bought a pool table and a Ping-Pong table. Best of all, we formed a soccer team, with practising rights to a major soccer field. We weren't very good, but we had a lot of fun.

I was called to attend an all-unions presidents' meeting, where all the union leaders had to report to the labour minister on any problems or needs in any of the trades. It was a great idea for the new communist government. All union presidents had to attend joint meetings three times a year; through the unions, the government controlled the whole country's labour force. I was amazed at how simply the government gained control. Each union was represented by their president, and the government controlled the union through the labour minister. One order from the minister could stop all trades in the country.

I was new and stupid and feeling important, and reported that a dental laboratory owner was using an apprentice to do his personal tasks. All apprentices had to sign a three-year contract agreeing to stay in the same place to learn, and the lab owners had to agree they would teach them and not use them for any other purpose. An apprentice had made a complaint to me, but the owner of the laboratory wouldn't listen to me. I thought that by reporting him maybe someone would talk to him and I would get the complaint solved. I was asked for the name of the lab, which I disclosed. A couple of days later the lab was broken into, causing damage to equipment and to partially finished work. Some people said the police had stood by and watched. I had learned a quick lesson on how communism worked.

The secretary of the union soon asked me to join the Communist Party. He said that every union president had to be a party member and that he would personally nominate me. I declined, stating I didn't know anything about communism, and that I couldn't join anything without knowing more about it. He thought I was wise, and he agreed to provide me with books about communism. I wanted to gain time because I was still planning to leave the country. Each time he saw me, he asked me how I was doing and if I was ready to join. I kept thinking up excuses, returning the books and asking for new ones, telling him that I was getting closer.

I had been taking English lessons because I knew that was the language spoken in the countries I was interested in immigrating to. I had also heard that in Palestine, English, Hebrew and Arabic were spoken. I remembered some of what the soldiers in Germany had started to teach me, and I found it was easy to learn English. In May 1948, the United Nations had voted to establish the State of Israel. Shortly after, someone from my Zionist organization told me to get ready to leave for Palestine on the next aliyah. We couldn't leave the country legally, but the movement had organized illegal ways to get out. The Arab states were attacking the new state and Israel needed every able-bodied person to join the fight. My sister, Magda, and I both wanted to go, but when we told my mother she started crying and wouldn't stop for days. She cried that we had lost our brother and that she would kill herself if one of us died in another war. We told her that we didn't want to live in Hungary any longer, and she finally agreed to let us go anywhere there was no war. We gave in to her wishes and decided not to go to Israel. We started to plan to go somewhere else.

One of my mother's cousins, Aladar, lived in the small village of Bodrogkeresztúr, where he was the head of the Jewish community. He came to visit us in Budapest, and we told him of our intentions to leave Hungary. He had just received information that Canada had agreed to allow 1,000 orphaned Jewish children under the age of eighteen to immigrate there. My cousin managed to get the name of a child, also named Miklos, who had lived in the village and died in the camps and using that name and identity, and my photo, he put in an application for me to go to Canada. My last name was now registered as Moskovits, and my age was listed as seventeen rather than nineteen. My brother and sister decided to come with me. I assured my parents that if we got to Canada, we would try and bring them over as soon as possible.

Our cousin paid the police to sign my passport application. He told us that the police didn't even look at the paper, just at how much money they were getting. In a surprisingly short time, we all got passports to leave for Canada. The emigration office wasn't busy because few people were allowed to leave the country – the so-called Iron Curtain was in place. Before we could get visas, we had to have a medical check-up at the department of health. Twelve of us took the test, and we all passed the first part of the health check. Then we had to give a urine sample. I tried and tried but I could not do it. Not wanting to come back some other time, I took some urine from Minyu, a girl who had a full glass. It was a good thing she was not pregnant! I saw a lot of people I knew in the building. When a man called out to me, "Hello Miklos," I was relieved that this was still my name.

When my travel visa was shipped to the police station in Bodrog-keresztúr, the chief of police called our cousin, asking him to explain. Aladar told him not to worry, that his own signature was on the paper and that the child, Miklos Moskovits, had died and no one would complain. Nonetheless, Aladar gave him a large sum of money to ensure I got my visa, which would allow me to leave the country.

In late September 1948, Fredi and I boarded a train to Paris, France. My sister had left a week earlier. I didn't say goodbye to anyone. I was at a meeting until 10:00 p.m. and stayed afterward, pretending to prepare for the next meeting.

When we reached the Austrian border, both a Hungarian and a Russian border guard came in to check our passports. In our compartment on the train, six of us were travelling with false papers. The Hungarian pointed to my suitcase and ordered me to open it. It happened to be the piece of luggage in which I was carrying a shoebox of cookies as a favour for a friend; I was taking it to his aunt who lived in Paris. I had asked my friend to be sure not to include any letters in the box, and he had promised he would not. Nonetheless, the Hungarian guard opened the box and found a letter sitting on top of the cookies. We were panicking, and I could already see us being taken back and put in jail. He started to read the letter and then stopped, folded it back the way it was, saluted and wished us a good trip. As soon as the guards left the compartment, I read the letter. It was full of glowing praise for the Communist government and stated that my friend's uncle was a high-ranking official. Looking through the window, we saw police taking people off the train and leading them into the station office. We were relieved when the train pulled out of the station. As the train crossed the border out of Hungary, I thought that I would never want to come back. One of the boys, Zoltan, had a flask of rum with him and offered everybody a drink to celebrate. The conductor came in and asked for a drink as well, also glad to have crossed the border.

When we arrived in Paris, a Hungarian-speaking woman was

waiting for us. She was a volunteer for the local Jewish organization, and she took us to a suburb of Paris called Jouy-en-Josas, where the former president of France, Léon Blum, owned a country house. The house was now being used as temporary shelter for children orphaned by the war, and many children were there when we arrived. The place was beautiful, located on the slope of a high hill. Four people shared one room, and there was a large dining room and a full kitchen with cooks and helpers. The food was tasty and we were treated as guests.

The first chance we had, Fredi and I took the local train to Paris, which was only a twenty-minute ride away. Fredi and I walked along the streets, eager to see the city. We saw a woman selling bananas and, having never tried them before, I wanted to buy some. We each had ten US dollars that our parents had given to us when we left Hungary. I didn't speak French, so I took out a one-dollar bill and pointed to the bananas. She filled up a bag with at least twelve of them. The dollar was very valuable in Europe and I hadn't wanted to spend the whole amount, but I didn't know how to ask for change and she wasn't offering any. We ate as many bananas as we could and left the rest on a bench. We spent the day just getting to know the city, walking mainly around the opera area, and also saw where the Louvre was; I marked in my book how to get back there. I looked around me and, for the first time, I felt free. It was a strange, beautiful city. Although I couldn't speak the language, I felt I was in a free country, not threatened by communists or Hungarian antisemites. I felt liberated.

The next time I went into Paris I delivered the cookies to my friend's aunt, who happened to be a young, pretty lady who spoke Hungarian. She was married to a much older wealthy Hungarian businessman who was away a lot. She was bored and had a lot of free time. When her husband came home that day he asked me to stay for lunch, and then suggested his wife take me out and show me the sights. She took me to the Folies Bergère and other tourist attractions. I was invited to come back, and did so frequently. Sometimes her husband came along on our outings, but he was happier if we went without him. I spent a lot of time with them and they treated me like a member of their family. As I got to know Paris, the weeks passed quickly. I spent a lot of time visiting museums. In the Louvre I spent days, yet still I saw only part of it. In the Musée d'Orsay, the museum that holds Impressionist works, I was fascinated by the paintings of Monet, Cézanne and Renoir. In Hungary, the museum had just a few paintings by the Impressionists, and now I could tell that they were inferior to those in Paris.

Fredi was having a great time with the other children. They were being supervised by qualified staff in the game rooms, which had Ping-Pong tables, and he learned to play quite well. A few Hungarian girls had decided to knit a sweater for me. The office provided the wool and they divided the work between them. When they were finished, with big fanfare, everybody got together to give me the sweater. I put it on and they all broke out in laughter. Apparently they had all used different knitting techniques and each part looked different. The front was tightly knitted, and one sleeve had big loops while the other was smooth. To me, the thought was more important. I told the girls I loved the sweater and would keep it forever.

We had been in Jouy-en-Josas for three months when one morning, the woman who had picked us up from the train station came and took the six of us to Paris to meet with the Canadian consul to try to obtain visas to go to Canada. We were all called into his office. The consul looked us over and said, "So, you guys want to go to Canada? Do you know that Canada is a tough, pioneer country? In Canada, expect to work hard, but if you do you will be able to live in freedom and be well rewarded." Then he pointed to my brother Fredi, who was the youngest, and called him over. He took out a bottle of whiskey from a cabinet and poured a small glass full. He said, "If you can drink this, you'll get your visas." Fredi picked up the glass and, just like he had seen in the movies, lifted it to his mouth and swallowed the whiskey with one motion. He didn't make a sound, but I saw tears in his eyes. We got our visas.

Le Havre to Hamilton

In December 1948, we boarded a ship called the *Scythia* and sailed from Le Havre to Halifax, Canada. There were children on the ship with us from almost every country in Europe. Fredi and I stayed on the top deck the whole time because a sailor friend of our father's told us that we wouldn't get seasick that way. We were practically the only ones who made it to the dining room for dinner – everyone else was seasick. One evening, the ship rocked so much that a table came loose and smashed into a wall of mirrors, covering the floor with glass. The weather was also getting much colder and we had to dig out our winter coats. I even put on my fancy knitted sweater.

Seven days later, we arrived at Pier 21 in Halifax. Most people disembarked, but we had to stay on board. More than fifty of us assembled on deck as a couple of photographers took our pictures and asked us, "Who is the one-thousandth among you?" We pushed the youngest-looking one forward and they took his picture separately. Some of the children were taken off, but a group of us had to stay on board.

Later on, some people from the Halifax Jewish community came and took us to a synagogue, where they had prepared a banquet to welcome us. They gave speeches telling us that we would have a wonderful life in Canada. After a delicious dinner, they drove us back to the ship. It was snowing and beautiful, and in a short time everything was white. There wasn't much traffic on the streets and it felt quiet and peaceful. We were told that we had to spend the night on the ship because we had to go through immigration in the morning. I was pleased with myself that I could understand so much more than I had thought I would. My evening English classes had been very helpful.

The next morning we disembarked and were placed into wire cages in a large reception hall. It made us feel like animals in a zoo. Thankfully, we didn't stay long in the cages. We were called out individually and, with little questioning, we got our passports stamped and were admitted into Canada.

We were then taken to the train station and given tickets for sleeper cars and for dinners in the dining car. We boarded the train to Montreal. Out the windows, all I could see was snow. The cars at the stations kept their engines running, I was told, to make sure that they would start. It looked so cold and there was so much snow that we were already talking about how we could get back to Europe! I sat with three others in the dining car, and a young girl who had been with us on the ship asked if she could eat with us. Naturally, we welcomed her. Her name was Trudy and she was all alone because her family had died in Auschwitz. She had survived by hiding as a gentile in a small city in France. She spoke English and I was glad that I could talk to her. I asked the waiter to bring us dinner because I wasn't familiar with the menu. He obliged and brought us a well-put-together, complete dinner. Some of our group at another table didn't speak English well and ordered three types of potatoes.

When we arrived in Montreal the next day, a couple of women were waiting for us from Montreal's Jewish community. They took us for dinner and then back to the railway station. My brother and I were going to Hamilton – one of our cousins, who lived in St. Thomas, had arranged this – and everybody else was going to Winnipeg. We said goodbye to our friends, but just before boarding, Trudy approached us. She explained that she refused to go to Winnipeg because she wanted to come with us. We were happy that we'd know someone in Hamilton.

Early that Sunday morning in Hamilton, a Hungarian-speaking woman was waiting for us. Her name was Mrs. Lukatch, and she told us that Fredi and I would be going to stay with the Rosenscheins in a very nice home where we were to receive room and board paid for by the Jewish congress. Trudy was to go with her until they found her a place to stay, as they had not been expecting her.

We were introduced to Mrs. Rosenschein and her two daughters. The older one was about my age and the other was younger, closer to Fredi's age. The father was not home, as he had gone to work early at a tailor shop. Mrs. Rosenschein said he'd be home soon for breakfast and to meet us, and then she told us how wonderful it was that some time in the future we could marry her daughters! I understood enough English to know what she had said, but I didn't translate for Fredi. I didn't know the customs here, but I was certainly not thinking about marriage.

As we started to eat breakfast, Mr. Rosenschein came in and joined us. They served a delicious breakfast – it was the first time we were introduced to bagels with cream cheese. What a wonderful combination. They were the most hospitable family, and had really been looking forward to meeting us. I, however, could sense problems. Their two daughters were so beautiful that we couldn't take our eyes off them. We couldn't get involved with them at this time. I was old enough to know that living in the same house, in the next room, would not work. I was twenty years old and I was not ready to get into trouble.

They showed us our room upstairs and we left our luggage there and went to find the Jewish community centre. There, we met Mr. Bradshaw, the director. He welcomed us to Hamilton, took us around the centre and told us it was always open for us. "Our city is glad to have survivor children come here," he said. "We already have six other orphaned Hungarian boys. They should be coming in a few minutes to meet you." Soon after, we met Robert, Leslie, Jack and Morris. Arnold and Dugyu joined us later. We were all friends immediately. Leslie already owned a car, and we all got in and went to see his place.

We met his hostess, Mrs. Stein, who told us to come by any time.

That afternoon, my mother's cousins Al and Ida Green, who lived in St. Thomas, came to see us. Al drove a brand new green Chrysler, which really impressed us. He took charge of us; he was the one who had arranged that we come to Hamilton, to be close to them. Uncle Al, as he told me to call him, asked us how the place they selected for us to stay was. I said that we liked the family but I was concerned that it would be difficult to live in the same house as the daughters, and that we'd prefer to stay with Mrs. Stein. He drove us to her home, and though she wasn't eager to take more boarders, Uncle Al promised her more money and she finally agreed, under the condition that we help wash dishes. I explained that I had never done this before, but I was willing to learn. We moved and Uncle Al apologized to the Rosenscheins for us leaving.

Unfortunately, on my second day at Mrs. Steins', I accidentally broke a plate. She forbade me to ever touch anything in the kitchen again. That left Fredi in the kitchen to help, which did not please him at all. He broke a plate the next day and was also forbidden to help in the kitchen. From then on, we all got along fine.

Our cousins' family was very welcoming. We went to St. Thomas for the weekend and met their three children, Mendel, Rochelle and Beryl. After that visit, we often went to see them on weekends. It was a surprise to me that on Sunday mornings we all went in to London, Ontario, for a Tefillin Club. I was used to going to the synagogue on Saturdays, on Shabbat, but Uncle Al explained that most people worked in stores and that Saturday was the busiest day for them.

The Hamilton Jewish centre was also very helpful. Anything we asked for, Mr. Bradshaw tried to accommodate. I told him that I had been going to dental school in Hungary, and he took me to the College of Dental Surgeons in Toronto, where they gave me an impromptu exam to find out how far I had gotten in my dental studies. They explained that I was the first foreign student they had seen and they had to evaluate me and decide where to place me. After, they called in Mr. Bradshaw and let him know that I had enough knowledge to enter the second year, but that my English was not sufficient for the university. They recommended I go back to pre-dents for a year, then come back to dentistry to continue with my studies. After receiving further information, we learned that pre-dents was only an extension of Grade 13. For that I was missing several subjects, including two English classes, so I decided against it. I knew that I would need private tutoring and have to go to school for several years and be supported through charity. I couldn't do that. I wanted to make money and bring our family together.

I got a temporary job in a factory that made porcelain for electric transformers. In the meantime, I looked for a job in dentistry. I soon found work in a laboratory for a dentist named Dr. Norman Simon. I loved the work and Dr. Simon was a terrific man. The only problem was that he wasn't paying me enough. When I asked for more money, he asked me why I needed it. I said I needed a new suit and he replied, "So go down to the menswear store, buy one and charge it to me." The next time I asked for more money, he asked me the same question. When I told him I wanted to go to the Toronto Exhibition, he agreed to take me. He brought his girlfriend along and he paid for everything, but he wouldn't pay me more money. I was earning twenty-five dollars a week while my friends were getting fifty dollars working in the Studebaker factory. I soon got an additional job with another dentist, Dr. David Siegel, and did his laboratory work in the evenings. He gave me a key to the office and left me instructions.

I spent some time with Trudy, who was staying with a wealthy lady, Mrs. Goldblatt. She was single and loved having Trudy stay with her. Trudy had a good home there and I visited often. Mrs. Goldblatt liked when I came over and she offered to pay for the wedding if I married Trudy. I didn't feel ready for that, and declined her generous offer. Much later, I was saddened to learn that Trudy couldn't get over losing her family in the war; she eventually spent time in a mental health hospital.

After a few months, I received a letter from my friend Zoltan, who had been living in Winnipeg. He didn't like it there and complained that the weather was so cold he had to cover his nose with his hand when he went outside. I managed to get him a job in a chocolate factory, and he and his nephew Emil moved to Hamilton.

My brother Fredi started to learn English and entered high school. We soon heard from our sister, Magda, who was in Vancouver. I wrote her, asking if she would come to Hamilton because we missed her. She answered that she would, if she could get work. I found her a job at the Lukatch travel agency. My sister could type and do shorthand in Hungarian and they needed her, so they paid the cost of the train to Hamilton.

Magda arrived in April 1949 with a Hungarian girl, Vera. They had become close friends and Vera hadn't wanted to stay in Vancouver without Magda. They met the rest of the Hungarian boys and it didn't take long for Vera and Robert to fall in love. A few months later, they married. We were all delighted for them, and happy to have another house where we could all get together. Having one of our people in their own home gave us a sense of permanence in Hamilton.

The older Jewish population of Hamilton was kind to us, but the younger generation, those our age, didn't want anything to do with us. The girls were snobbish and wouldn't date us. They thought dating "greeners" – as they referred to us – was below their class. If we wanted to date Jewish girls, we had to go to Toronto. Eventually, we all married girls from somewhere else. I married a girl from Toronto, Fredi a girl from New York, Zoltan one from Montreal and Dugyu one from Paris. In later years one of the Hamilton Jewish women asked me, "How come you boys did not marry girls from Hamilton?" I reminded her how we had been treated by the girls. She said they were sorry about it now.

～

When we left Hungary, I thought that we had left antisemitism behind. But I was mistaken. On a drive to Toronto on Highway 2, in the suburbs of Lorne Park, I saw an old sign that said, "Jews and dogs not allowed." It was the old Canada. Jews had never been welcomed with open arms. In 1939, when a ship called the *St. Louis* had tried to land in Canada with Jewish refugees escaping from Germany, the government refused it; the ship was forced to return to Europe and many on board later perished under Nazi occupation. I mentioned this once to Mr. Bradshaw and his answer was, "There is a difference. Here, we had the will and the right to fight back." And he told me about the Christie Pits riots in 1933, when Jewish and Italian youth joined together and fought the local Nazi party for six hours. Apparently hundreds of people fought, and the police didn't get involved. Mostly, they just stood by.

Canada had long since become, for the most part, an immigrant-friendly country. In Toronto today, approximately 50 per cent of the population are immigrants. All those people living side by side, different areas populated by diverse ethnic groups. In some places, the street signs are even in their native language.

During our first two summers, we often went to Burlington Beach. On the street by the beach a store sold ice creams, hot dogs and milkshakes; it always had long lineups and I thought it must be a decent business. At the end of the summer of 1949, I noticed a for-sale sign in the store window and just for fun, I went in and asked how much the owner wanted for it. He said that for the house, which had two bedrooms, the business and the equipment, he was asking $1,500. I thought the price was pretty reasonable. I realized that the store wasn't in the city, but I thought I'd make the money back in no time. I told the owner I was willing to buy it, but I didn't have all the money and that, if he agreed to wait until next summer, when I was making money, I could pay him as I earned it. I also thought I could borrow a couple hundred dollars from Uncle Al, and that by the fall I would have saved another hundred and I would manage. The owner accepted my offer because he wanted to get out of the seasonal business.

I gave him my one hundred dollars of savings as a deposit, we made a contract and I took it to a lawyer, Mr. Harold Minden, who was connected to the Jewish community centre. I knew that I was being impulsive, that I should have investigated a bit before making an offer, but I felt that because I had nothing, I had nothing to lose. Two weeks later, Mr. Minden called and advised me not to go through with the purchase because the deed was no good. He said the owner of the building had died and left it in his will to his infant son, who was now about thirty years old and living a few blocks away. His mother had forged her son's signature on the deed, but if he ever found out he could probably reclaim it in court. I went back to the seller, explaining the situation, and asked for my deposit back. He claimed he hadn't known about the deed and didn't blame me for backing out, but he had already spent the money. Instead of my deposit, he gave me his car. I had no other choice, so I took the car. I now owned a 1935 Ford. It had a wooden floor and a leaking canvas roof, but to me it was great. Now I really needed to make more money – I wasn't earning enough to support either me or my car.

In the building where Dr. Simon had his office there was a kiosk selling magazines, baked goods and cigarettes. The owner wanted to sell, so I borrowed some money from Mr. Lukatch and bought it and operated it for a couple of months. I was making more than I was working for Dr. Simon, but I realized it was not a future for me, and resold it for a little more money. I repaid the loan from Mr. Lukatch, who wouldn't take any interest from me.

It was difficult to find a well-paying job. Finally, at some point in 1950, Mr. Lukatch got me a better-paying job in the Steel Company of Canada as a furnace man. It was hard work. I had to use a sledgehammer to break up large pieces of zinc into sizes that could be picked up and put into the furnace. On my first day, a French-Canadian man working nearby called out, "Now they are hiring dirty Jews." I lost my temper and picked up the sledgehammer by me and threw it at him. He ducked, and the hammer smashed into the corrugated steel wall. The whole factory shook. Everybody ran over to ask what had happened. I told them that I had left Europe because of the antisemitism and that I wouldn't stand for anybody ever again calling me a dirty Jew. The foreman said to the French-Canadian man, "If you open your filthy mouth again, I, not Mike, will kill you."

The work continued to be tough. When I had to work with melting copper, pouring it in moulds, it was so hot and smelly that we worked only ten minutes, then we had ten minutes outside to cool off. We looked like spacemen, wearing goggles, facemasks and long leather gloves. One day they hired a large Canadian man; he must have weighed 230 pounds. After working only one hour he quit, commenting that it was worse than jail. Except for the foreman, all the workers were immigrants. I worked there for six months and didn't encounter any more antisemitism. I was treated with respect, the pay was very good and I managed to save some money.

That year, my sister met a nice young man named Mort Guzner, who worked with his parents at the grocery store they owned. They fell in love and got married. When they moved into his mother's large house, which had several bedrooms, Fredi and I moved in as well and we all enjoyed living there together.

Fredi had a part-time job in a gas station, which helped us to save some money. By the end of the year, I felt we were settled and that it was time to write to our parents and plan to bring them to Canada. In my letter to them, I suggested that they go to Germany and visit "Mr. Markus and Serena Moskovits." I was sure that they would understand my intentions to register under different names, as the parents of the person listed on my false identity documents. They did, and wrote back that they had gone to Újhely – where my father used to own the tavern – and, with Gyula's help, had gotten into Czechoslovakia. From there, they managed to get over to a DP camp in Germany. At the camp, they registered as Markus and Serena Moskovits and then wrote me a letter, informing me of their arrival. With that information, I went to the immigration office and reported that I had found my parents alive in Germany and wanted to bring them to Canada. I was questioned as to how and I said it was them that located me, that they had been reading a Jewish newspaper and saw a story that Canada had accepted 1,000 orphaned children and that a boy with the last name Moskovits was one of them. I told them I had received a letter from them, asking if I could possibly be their son. The immigration officer asked me to bring the letter, so we put a letter in an envelope from Germany. The immigration office checked the watermark on the letter and accepted the claim.

Businessmen

In the summer of 1951, my parents and my brother George received visas to come to Canada. We drove to Toronto to pick them up at the train station. It was so wonderful to see them get out of the train, looking so well. My father could not believe it when he saw that I owned a car; in Hungary, only the very wealthy owned cars. On the highway he kept asking me to drive faster, to see how fast the car could go.

We rented a temporary flat for them in Hamilton while my father looked for a job. He went to a Jewish agency for help but because he didn't speak English, he couldn't find work. On Shabbat, somebody in the synagogue suggested he buy scrap iron from farmers and then sell it to the scrapyard. I realized that was a good idea since I was also looking for something else to do. Working in the steel company was no future for me.

I bought a used Studebaker truck with my savings, and we went out to try our new venture. People were happy to sell old stoves and other scrap lying around. I had no idea how much to pay, so I asked how much they wanted and paid what they asked. By 4:00 p.m. the first day, when we took our load to the scrapyard, I had made more money than I was getting paid for a week's work in the factory. We were in business. We continued buying scrap iron for quite a few months, venturing farther and farther into the countryside. We bought bigger items like old tractors, broken farm equipment. We worked hard, loading the truck every day, but our income was high and we were travelling a lot and meeting people on the farms. I found rural people quite friendly; in several places they insisted that we eat some "good country food, not like you eat in the city." Most of the farmers we met said they would never live in the city. They felt that the traffic and the noise would make their lives miserable.

We saved our money until we decided we had enough to look for a better place to live. At a real estate office, an agent sized us up as two newcomers. He asked us how much money we had and we told him two thousand dollars. He said he had the perfect house for us and took us to a two-storey house on Cumberland Street. It was empty and we thought it was big enough for the family; we both liked it. When I inquired about some railroad tracks behind the garden's fence, the agent said it was nothing, just a side track occasionally used to push some cars out of the way. We went back to the office, asked how much the seller wanted, and paid the exact price – six thousand dollars. We never thought to offer less than the asking price. We went home proudly to tell my mother that we had bought her a house. She said, "What? You bought a house without me seeing it?" She was skeptical at first, but she liked it too. We moved in and were hardly there an hour when a train went by, shaking the cupboard doors open. It was the main line from Toronto to Buffalo! I felt foolish and promised myself to be more careful in the future.

After living in the house for one year we sold it for a couple of thousand more than we had bought it for. I realized that was a good way to make money in Canada. After being in the scrap business for some time, we happened to go through the village of Simcoe, where we saw an autowreck yard. I went in and asked the owner, Mr. Blayne, if he had any scrap cars to sell. In the backyard, there were more than a hundred cars in different conditions – broken pieces, motors missing, doors and transmissions everywhere. It was overwhelming. This was the biggest amount of scrap we had considered. I spent time estimating how much to offer, then decided on three thousand dollars. He accepted the deal and we gave him five hundred dollars as a deposit. After supper, thinking about the deal, I realized that I had offered the price that the scrap was worth as is, not considering profit or the amount of work we had to put in for cutting it up and taking it to a Hamilton scrapyard. I couldn't sleep all night.

First thing in the morning, we drove to Simcoe and I told Mr. Blayne my mistake. I apologized and said that if I had to lose the deposit I would, but that we'd be working for months without earning any money, and would lose money on gas and other expenses. Mr. Blayne said, "You are the first honest scrap dealer I have ever met. You go ahead and take a load every day, and whatever you get you will know how much to give me." We worked there for two months and became close friends with his whole family. He was extremely pleased with the amount he was receiving, and we were satisfied as well.

By the time we were finished in Simcoe, I was experienced in cutting and evaluating scrap cars. We started to look for other wrecking yards and found a much bigger one in Welland. I introduced myself to the owner as a specialist in scrapyards who cleared the unsaleable remnants of old cars. Ed, the owner, invited me out for a few beers to discuss the deal. He ordered six beers to start, took three and pushed the other three at me. I couldn't drink more than one to his three, and when he went to the washroom I quickly changed his empties and put my two full ones in front of him. I told him I'd ordered him a couple more. I made a deal with him so big that we couldn't do it on our own; it was three times more than what we had in Simcoe. By this time, I didn't want my father and I to work as hard. I went to the steel company and made arrangements for them to go to Welland and load trailers to take the scrap cars back to the yard. They paid me for the scrap and I paid them for the transportation. With cranes and tractor trailers, it still took three weeks to haul everything to Hamilton.

After that job, I took the train to New York for a holiday. I enjoyed my time there with my friend Bandi, one of the five twins from Hungary, who moved there after I left Budapest. We went to theatres, museums and great restaurants. I thought the life in New York too hectic, but it was exciting to visit. I was amazed at the size of the buildings in the city. Paris was also a cosmopolitan city, but without those huge skyscrapers.

When I got back, my father was waiting for me at the railway station, and with a big smile, he said, "I got a surprise for you. You bought a house." I replied, "Oh no." He told me not to worry, that it had two apartments and we'd collect rent. I hadn't wanted to buy a house – I'd had other plans – but there was nothing I could do about it. He had signed the papers and the lawyer said it was legal. At the end of the month, we sent my brother Fredi, who was now working in an autoparts store close to the house, to collect the first month's rent. When he came home, he told us that when he went in, a lady said, "Please sit down, she will be with you in a minute." Fredi waited and saw a man come out of a room, followed by a woman wearing only a see-through housecoat. When Fredi was inside the room the woman asked him, "How do you want it?" He said, "In cash. I am here to collect the rent." She started to laugh and called in the other woman, who paid him. By this time, he had figured out that it was a whorehouse. We tried to sell it, but nobody would even go to see it. Hamilton was a small city and most people knew the house's reputation.

I quit the scrap business and left it to my father. I had never liked the business; it was a money-maker, but I hated the dirty, hard work. I wanted to go back into dentistry. I realized that in Hamilton I had little opportunity to find a job in that profession, but I wanted to gain some more Canadian experience in dentistry, so in the fall of 1953 I went to Toronto, where I knew some Jewish boys. They encouraged me to move there, and the house my friend Leslie lived in even had a room available for me to stay in. I rented a furnished room and moved in, hoping I would have a better chance of working in dentistry in Toronto.

In the newspaper I found the largest dental laboratory, went there and spoke to the manager. He questioned my qualifications and then said he didn't need anybody presently, but that he would recommend me to the dental college. They were looking for someone qualified in every facet of laboratory work as an instructor. I went to apply for the position and handed my resumé to a receptionist. I noticed that the minute he saw my name, Moskovits, he stopped reading and told me they would let me know if a job became available. He just handed me back my resumé and didn't even ask for my phone number. I was disappointed. I thought about how when I came in to apply for the job, he had asked for my resumé. So, a few days later, I went back and reapplied as Michael Mason. (I had been reading a Perry Mason book and that had given me the idea for the name.) I was immediately taken in to see the head of the department, who offered me the position, subject to a three-day trial period.

For three days, I worked in the lab with the head technician, with whom I got along. He assured me I would get the job. I liked the place and the working environment. The afternoon of the third day, the head of the prosthodontics department gave me a small test. He called in a student from the graduating year, asked him to bring in his denture work and gave it to me to evaluate. I thought it was very bad. Thinking that if I said how bad it was, the student would get poor marks, I said it needed corrections and it would be easier if he started from the beginning. The department head looked at me and smiled. After conferring with the head technician, he told me I was hired.

I was offered a reasonable salary and four weeks of paid vacation. I accepted the position and followed the department head into his private office to sign the agreement. As he was writing up the contract, he asked me my name, address, schooling and then, what my religion was. I said I was Jewish. He stopped writing and looked at me. "You are Jewish?" I answered, "Yes, is that a problem?" He said, "No, but don't come in Monday because I have to bring it up with the board. I will call you." I never heard from him again. I realized that antisemitism was tolerated in Canada. I resented it, but I kept my name as Mason.

That same year, I took another job in a laboratory, worked for some time and then prepared for the exams required to open my own laboratory. By law, you had to have a licence to own a dental laboratory. I needed four years of Canadian experience to qualify for the exams, some of which I had previously gotten in Hamilton. The exam was difficult because you had to be qualified in every aspect of laboratory work. I had a wide variety of experience from Hungary, but in Canada, people gained experienced in only one phase of the work they specialized in, like making dentures, while another was strictly a gold technician or an orthodontic technician. I noticed that the other applicants did not know how to finish all the requirements. Two weeks after taking the exam, I received a letter informing me that I had passed, along with an invitation to the Royal York Hotel for a special dinner to receive the diploma. I found out that I was the first foreign-born applicant to meet the qualifying requirements.

⁓

At the end of December, my father called and asked me to come home for New Year's Eve. When I asked why, he replied, "Do not ask, just do what I tell you." I arrived home to guests in our living room, a family of Hungarian-Jewish tobacco farmers we had met a while back when we were out buying scrap near Tillsonburg. I had met their twenty-one-year-old daughter only once, and now here was her father asking me to take her out for dinner and dancing. He handed me pre-paid tickets for the whole evening. What could I do? We went. At midnight, the lights went out and she kissed me. She was fine-looking, but just not my type. When we got home, my father said, "It is all set – you marry her and for a wedding present you will get from them a tobacco farm near Tillsonburg." I was speechless. Did my father think we were still in Europe in the Middle Ages? He was trying to sell me for a tobacco farm! I almost started to laugh, but politely excused myself instead, claiming that I had a headache. We never heard from the family again.

At the beginning of 1954, my father called and asked me to come home because he had bought a small supermarket in Fort Erie. He wanted me to come run the business. I quit my job at the dental laboratory, which I regretted; I liked the people who worked there. I moved to Fort Erie and became a grocer. The previous owner, Mr. George, was Hungarian, and he stayed for three months to teach us the business. He was a butcher by trade, made his own sausages and corned beef, and had a lot of Hungarian customers from the area. Business was good, and I thought my father had done well this time. After the three months, customers stopped coming. I was sure they did not want to buy from a Jewish store. Also, an A& P store opened two doors away. It took us another four months to lose the store, and we still owed Mr. George six thousand dollars. I told him we didn't have the money but that I owned a house in Hamilton worth that amount, and if he wanted, he could have it. He agreed without going to see it, and that's how we got rid of the whorehouse.

There were no Jewish girls in Fort Erie and I was lonely, so on Saturday nights I drove back to Toronto. My friends all had dates, so I looked in my book and called a girl named Ruth, whose number Aunty Ida had given me. She turned out to be lovely, and I came in to see her a few more weekends, but it was far from Fort Erie to Toronto, to come for a few hours. I told her I would see her when I moved back to Toronto, and I moved back after we lost the store. I was glad to be back, and I renewed my relationship with Ruth, whom everybody called Ricky. We had a lot of fun together. She was a very intelligent girl, trained as a schoolteacher, and she taught English to Grade 5 students. She was a good writer, too, and had won a major Canadian writing contest. She was determined to correct the way I spoke English. Under her influence, I attended some university lectures, mainly about art appreciation. In July 1954, after a few months of dating, we got married. Our wedding was beautiful; my brother Fredi was my best man and my sister, Magda, was a bridesmaid.

When we returned to the city from our honeymoon in Muskoka, I decided it was time to open a dental laboratory. I went to see a major dental supply company and asked them to show me on a map the locations of all the dental laboratories in the city. With that information, I selected the Lakeshore area in Mimico, a suburb of Toronto. Not having much money, I rented a basement on Lakeshore Boulevard. I met a Hungarian-Jewish dentist who had just emigrated from Israel and asked him to be my business partner. Mr. Ervin Pollak was a quality technician with a lot of experience, and I needed someone to do the work while I was out visiting dentists to try and get their business. Ricky and I rented a modest apartment, bought some furniture and moved in. It felt wonderful to have our own apartment, start a new business, have our own destiny.

I met another laboratory owner in Toronto, Mr. Nagy, who was very helpful when I told him I was opening my own laboratory. He explained how much difficulty he had had when he started, and he offered to help us with anything that he could. He gave me advice as well as surplus materials and some older equipment that he wasn't using anymore. We bought used furniture and did all the electrical wiring and plumbing ourselves. However, the supply houses weren't giving us any credit. I overheard one salesman saying, "I give them three months before they close down." It was a slow growth for us, but our business improved gradually; we did quality work and provided quick, efficient service. We were recommended to other offices and we became the established lab in the area. Eventually, we grew more successful and employed four other technicians.

The Lakeshore didn't have a large Jewish population and my clients were mostly gentile. On Yom Kippur, we decided to close for the holiday. When I told one of my clients, whom I had become friends with, that we would be closed for the Jewish holiday, he was shocked and exclaimed, "I did not know that you were Jewish!" Our wives had become friends too, meeting regularly, but he quit us the same day. Once again I realized that, though hidden, antisemitism was still alive in Toronto.

Eventually, we moved and rented a larger space in an office building. At street level was a small snack bar owned by a German woman, Hilda. It was conveniently located and we often had our coffees and lunch there. One day my younger brother George came visiting and I asked him to go down and bring us some drinks. When he came back, his face was pale and he was upset. I asked him what was wrong and he told me that a man in the snack bar had said, "The only trouble with Hitler was that he did not kill all the Jews." I had always had a short temper, but this time I really lost it. I ran down to the shop and saw four people seated at the counter. I jumped over the counter, grabbed a big knife from the server, got on top of the counter and yelled, "Who was the bastard who said Hitler did not kill enough Jews?!" while waving the knife in my hand. It got deadly quiet. Hilda begged me, "Please, Mike, it was a misunderstanding, nobody said that." I said, "It better be, or I will send that person to meet Hitler." I threw the knife down and walked out. Upstairs, I told my colleagues that I didn't want anybody going to that snack bar anymore.

～

We had our first child in 1955, a lovely girl whom we named Robin. We thought we were in heaven. We had everything we wanted. As time went on we had three more children – Andrew, Tov and Roseanne. I really thought that God was trying to make up for my previous suffering. We bought a nice house not too far from our lab, which was close enough to go home for lunch and see the children.

The only problem was that there were no Jewish people or synagogues nearby. We decided to try to do something about it. Ricky called the Canadian Jewish Congress and requested the names of all the Jewish people who lived in the west suburbs of Toronto. We called all those people and asked them to come to our house to meet with other Jewish people who were interested in forming a Jewish community in our area. We had a turnout of thirty families, and they all agreed that we should form the West Suburban Jewish Community Association.

I was the first president and, from that, I became a member of the Canadian Jewish Congress. Our member Avy Siegel formed a Sunday Hebrew school and taught the children every week. All the parents were pleased that their children were getting a Jewish education.

When our daughter Robin entered the local public school, she came home crying. She told us that during the religion classes, as the only Jewish child, she was told she could wait outside. My wife called the principal, who suggested that Robin come to his office during that time. That didn't work out, because by being sent to the principal's office, Robin felt she was being punished.

In 1962, we decided to move into the city, to a more Jewish area. We bought a house on Duncannon Drive, and all of us were happy with the move. Financially we were all right, and our children were bright and healthy. We bought a country house and we worked at it with our children. We had wonderful times together, travelled a lot and saw many beautiful places.

Remembrance

In 1967, Ricky talked me into going back to Hungary. She wanted to see where I came from. I really didn't want to go back, but to please her, I agreed.

I was unsure about crossing the border into Hungary, but it wasn't a problem. The official hardly looked at my passport. We arrived in Budapest and checked in to the Hotel Gellért, which was built in 1918 during the Turkish occupation of Hungary. We rented a car and started our visit by going to my old apartment. There still wasn't an elevator and we had to walk up three floors. I knocked and an old woman let us in. I was surprised to find that everything was the same as it was when we had lived there. Our furniture, our carpets, even our painting on the wall. Nothing had changed. The woman explained that the government had given her the apartment and that she had no money to buy anything new. I bought her a bag of groceries. She was so poor that, although she wanted to serve us a glass of tea, she did not have enough tea or sugar.

From there, we went to see my former school; there, too, everything looked the same. Some street names had been changed and there were some new buildings, but otherwise Budapest was the same city. However, the attitude of the Jewish people seemed different. I felt they were more confident and more open in their Judaism than before. Many young men wore *kippahs* on the street, which was unheard of in my time.

We went to see the Dohány synagogue, which was going to be renovated. The building was still impressive, and we were told that the inside would be as beautiful as it used to be. The government was helping financially with the restorations. We did some sightseeing in the Jewish area, which seemed active, with a lot of storefronts bearing Hebrew lettering. Then we attended Sabbath services in the Kazinczy synagogue, which was more Orthodox than what we were used to in Toronto.

Although it seemed like the Jewish people felt secure in Budapest, in my opinion, there were disturbing signs that indicated otherwise. Most Hungarians had grown up around antisemitism. When I asked some people about antisemitism in the country, they all said, "I do not know about it; I have Jewish friends." I find the attitude of Hungarian people to be always extreme. When the Nazis were in Hungary, many citizens tried to be more Nazi than the Germans. Then, when the Russians occupied the country, they tried to be more communist than the Russians.

Then we left the city to go to the countryside, to my paternal grandparents' house in Abaújkér, which is about two hundred kilometres away. The house was now divided among three families. The people thought we were there to reclaim the property, and although I told them that I only wanted to see the place, they wouldn't let us in.

Next we went to find the Jewish cemetery. A couple of people I asked claimed there was no such thing there. At the church, the priest told me where the cemetery used to be. We found the place overgrown with weeds and the tombstones all gone, except for my grandfather's. Apparently my father's surviving brother, Uncle Zoltan, had paid for a new stone, which is why it was the only one standing. Uncle Zoltan had had all the names of our family members who had died engraved on the same stone.

There were no Jews living in the village. When I was a kid and I went to synagogue with my grandfather, there were more than thirty families at the service. I felt unwelcome in the village and, in general,

I wondered why Jews would want to live in Hungary. My wife thoroughly enjoyed the trip. For me, it was a reaffirmation of the wise choice I'd made to live in Canada.

Ricky wrote a weekly column in a newspaper, and she asked me whether I would mind if she wrote about our trip. I thought it might be interesting to read about how a Canadian woman reacted to her husband's birthplace. I told her I didn't mind so long as she wrote about the way she saw the trip, and not the way I did. When we returned home, she wrote the following article, which was published in the newspaper.

With me at his side, my husband returned to his birthplace. Was Thomas Wolfe correct when he said, "You can't go home again"? I feel a little apprehensive and am watching him closely. We make a private pilgrimage to the Dohány synagogue. It is a magnificent Moorish building. First, we are going upstairs to see the museum. It contains beautiful ritual objects – Kiddush cups, seder plates of Bohemian china, silver embroideries. A young visitor solemnly pointing to one particularly ornate silver Torah crown explains in Hungarian to his companion that it is the crown the Jewish priest wears. We stand a long time, examining the collection of photographs, newspapers, posters. "Do not deal with Jews," warns a poster depicting an accusing finger. Others show ugly caricatures. Silently we search the faces in the photographs taken in railway stations. They all seem vaguely familiar. They are Jewish faces. I see the same Jewish eyes in the photographs of recent bar mitzvah boys, of Jewish brides, of the celebrants at Chanukah and Purim festivals. There seems to be a healthy resurgence of Jewish life in Budapest. The synagogue holds regular services and has good attendance. A cabinet houses a moving memorial to the Hungarian Jews who perished in the Holocaust. My husband pauses to take a photograph in the courtyard before continuing on. The visit becomes an intense emotional experience for both of us.

Life seems to be quite cheerful for everyone. On Sunday, the zoo and lovely surrounding parks are filled with happy families. Rovers enjoy the pond in the park, and diners still enjoy the famous palachinta in chocolate sauce in the garden of the long-established Gundel restaurant. The waiter says, "Please command me, dear sir," and, "Kiss your hand, madam." I don't understand a word of all this. I smile, I hope graciously. My companion laughs out loud. There are many complaints, mostly about the lack of money. The Russians are said to be around, but they keep a low profile. Perhaps the Hungarian attitude is summed up by this comment by an elegant couple. "The Turks temporarily occupied us for one hundred and fifty years, the Germans for less than one, and the Russians are here temporarily for almost forty." Caviar and real pâté de foie are readily available, at one dollar eighty a serving; we certainly indulged but that is still expensive for Hungarians. Another day we dine at a Hungarian restaurant amidst marble and gilt opulence befitting an opera house at the turn of the century. My husband remembers another evening there many years ago. They had put all their money together but could afford only one bottle of wine for five of them. I see them, five brash, young hopefuls, hair slicked, best suits, ties of course. A diner at the next table had sent a bottle of wine over with the message, "Please invite my daughter to dance," so they had two bottles. Tonight, the diner at the next table is in shirtsleeves and carries a plastic shopping bag. He appears a strange contrast to the gilt columns. Life in Hungary still has the old style of elegance.

~

In 1973, I passed an examination at the Dental College and became a denturist. I opened an office and fit patients with dentures. One day, one of our frequent clients, Dr. Zickerman, who was Hungarian-born but lived and was educated in Toronto, asked me to make a set of dentures for his mother. He brought her to my office. While I was working, I asked her where she had lived in Hungary. To my surprise, she mentioned the village of Bodrogkeresztúr, where my mother's cousin had gotten the name for my passport. I asked her maiden name and she answered, "Moskovits." I didn't think that there could have been another family named Moskovits in that small village. My next question was, "Did you have a brother named Miklos?" She turned pale and asked me how I knew. I told her that I had arrived in Canada by borrowing her dead brother's name, and that my parents were here with her parents' names. She started crying and it took her son a while to calm her down. They had known me only by the name Mason, not Moskovits.

It is unbelievable that Miklos's surviving sister would come to Canada and one day arrive at my office in Toronto. She could have lived anywhere else in the world. I think that the chance of this happening must be one in many millions. But it did happen. Dr. Zickerman told this story to his rabbi on the occasion of his son's bar mitzvah. The rabbi spoke of the Jewish custom of naming a newborn child after a family member who has passed away, so that the name lives on. By carrying on the name of Miklos Moskovits, I became an honorary member of their family. We grew to be close friends and were invited to their simchas, as part of the family. Decades later, when our grandson Jacob Wagner had his bar mitzvah, he "twinned" – that is, he had it in honour of – Miklos Moskovits, who had died in Auschwitz before he reached the age of thirteen. Both families attended, and Yad Vashem gave us a certificate to honour the occasion.

~

In 1980, an ad in the *New York Times* caught my attention. It read, "If you would like to help Raoul Wallenberg, the Swedish diplomat who saved Jewish lives, call this number." I remembered the name from the stories my mother had told me so long ago in Bótrágy, when I came back from Germany, about being saved by him. Wallenberg had given protective Swedish passports to Jews who managed to get to the Swedish legation in Budapest. My mother had told me that because she had a baby, she could never get to the legation in time. She tried several times without success, arriving when the line was already too long. When she tried yet again and the same thing happened, she started to cry in frustration. On the other side of the wrought-iron fence, Wallenberg was walking in the garden. He stopped and asked her why she was crying. She explained that by the time she got the baby ready, the line in front of the legation had grown too long to get a passport. He asked her, "For whom do you need passports?" She gave him the names, and he went inside and came back out with passports for the family.

Wallenberg saved approximately 100,000 Hungarian Jews. When he arrived in Budapest in July 1944, his mission was to try to save some of the Hungarian Jews, and he had received American financial support for that purpose. He opened an office separate from the consulate and gave out thousands of temporary Swedish passports, called *Schutzpass*, to any Jewish person. He rented apartment buildings, put Swedish flags on them, and people with Swedish passports were then allowed to move into the apartments, which were safe houses. The consul from Switzerland also issued at least 8,000 Swiss passports, and is credited with saving close to 60,000 Hungarian Jews.

As the Soviet army approached Budapest, Wallenberg discovered that the Hungarian Arrow Cross, the fascist party, was planning to blow up the Budapest ghetto, which had about 80,000 people in it. Wallenberg went to the German army general in Budapest and told him that if he did not put a stop to it, Wallenberg personally would have him hanged as a war criminal after the war. The general ordered the German Wehrmacht army to stop the Hungarians from blowing up the ghetto. However, when the Soviets liberated Budapest, Wallenberg was taken into custody. He apparently told his driver, "I do not know if I am to be decorated or arrested." He was arrested and taken to the Soviet Union.

Later, I heard that the Russians considered Wallenberg an American spy. In 1947, when the Swedish government asked the Soviet government Wallenberg's whereabouts, they were told that he had died of a heart attack. As Wallenberg was still in his early thirties, this did not sound plausible.

I decided to help if I could. I called the telephone number, which was from Washington, DC, expecting to hear a request for donations. Instead, I was talking to Californian congressman Tom Lantos, also a Holocaust survivor, who invited me to come to Washington if I wanted to help. My wife and I went to Washington and met the congressional representative and his wife at the capitol. After having lunch there, we were introduced to Senator Tip O'Neill, the chairman of the senate. They asked us to represent the Wallenberg cause in Canada. We accepted and said we would do our best. We then received a letter from Sweden from Wallenberg's half-sister, Nina Lagergren, thanking us and promising help if we needed it. Coincidentally, the Swedish ambassador to Canada for the previous three years had been Per Anger, who was the secretary of the Swedish legation in Budapest during the German occupation of Hungary. We got in touch with him and he visited us in Toronto and offered his assistance. Per Anger and I travelled to Montreal and other places, where we made several speeches about Wallenberg's heroic efforts.

In Canada at that time, the Wallenberg name was not known or recognized except by a few government officials. Our goal was to get every Canadian to know his name and his accomplishment of saving so many innocent lives. His name is a testament to the fact that, with total commitment, one man accomplished more than some countries did with all their resources. Wallenberg defied both Eichmann and a German general. His name will go down in history as a man of courage and a great humanitarian.

Although, according to the Soviets, Wallenberg had died in 1947, much later, rumours circulated that he was still alive and being held in jail in Russia. Our neighbour Ellie Tesher was a reporter for the *Toronto Star*, and I approached her and told her the Wallenberg story. She was interested and followed up by interviewing my mother in Hamilton. She then wrote a major story in the *Star* about Wallenberg's heroic activities in Hungary during the last months of the war. The story created a lot of interest, and calls from other Hungarian survivors followed; we also received a lot of information from Russian immigrants that Wallenberg was still alive. Our goal was to create a lot of publicity so that perhaps the Russians would release him from prison. We spent a lot of time and money on the cause. Unfortunately, if he was still alive, nothing resulted in his release.

During our involvement, I received a call from a man who claimed to be an ex-Russian KGB colonel. He asked me to come to his apartment in Toronto and said he would give me all the information I wanted about Wallenberg. I called Mr. Per Anger in Ottawa, who was concerned for our safety, and he sent an embassy car with the Swedish flag on it, as well as an embassy person to accompany us on the visit.

The colonel had a camera set up on a tripod and took our picture. Then he told us he was the officer who had taken Mr. Wallenberg to Vladimir prison, and that he had no further useful information. He instead tried to talk to us about Stalin's atrocities against the Soviet soldiers who had been prisoners of war in Germany. We refused to listen and left without having gained any information that could advance our cause.

We did everything possible to promote the Wallenberg cause. Ricky took charge and formed a committee of professors from the University of Toronto and nominated Wallenberg for the Nobel Peace Prize, which unfortunately he did not get. We gave a writer the background information for a feature movie to be made in Hollywood, and we had several streets in different cities named in his honour. In Toronto, the street going into Earl Bales Park was named Raoul Wallenberg Road. In 1996, a memorial plaque was erected, and a tree was planted there. Eventually, Wallenberg became a household name in Canada. In 1985, Wallenberg was named an honorary Canadian citizen.

In 1989, long after the Khrushchev era, Per Anger and Nina Lagergren were called to Russia and given Wallenberg's belongings, including his passport. I think they accepted the fact that he was dead. I considered that we had done all that we could, and gave up any further effort. It had been an interesting experience in intrigue and politics.

~

My favourite times were Sunday mornings reading the *Canadian Jewish News*. In the summer of 1982, one article in particular aroused my interest. An Israeli family was looking to exchange their Jerusalem house for a house in Toronto for a few months. I thought about it and talked it over with Ricky. We decided it was worth investigating, and ended up making the arrangements, including exchanging cars. We flew over at the same time as the family was flying to Toronto, so we never met. In Israel, their large apartment overlooked the Knesset, the parliament. They had left us flowers, a bottle of champagne and a cake. From this welcome, we knew they were a nice family.

Later the same day, we received a call from their relatives, who lived in a kibbutz close to the Lebanese border. They invited us for Shabbat and we accepted; we had a wonderful experience of kibbutz living and communal work. Our hosts were Hungarian immigrants and they welcomed us like part of their family. The kibbutz was a well-established place with a large swimming pool. We spent a great weekend with them.

Back in Jerusalem, we called former Israeli Attorney-General Gideon Hausner, whom we had been in touch with through our involvement with the Wallenberg situation. He had invited us to visit him in Israel. Unfortunately, he was in the hospital and could not see us, but instead he arranged a private appointment with then president Yitzhak Navon in his home. When we arrived at the house a guard took our passports, and the president's secretary came out and invited us in. She told us that the president had had to leave and had instructed her to show us around, which she graciously did. We spent about an hour in the main lobby looking at the various presents that had been given to the president by different countries. By law, they were all property of Israel.

We stayed in Israel for the summer and lived like the Israelis – shopping, cooking at home and visiting friends. We loved every minute of our stay. In Jerusalem, we felt both at home and back in history. It felt as though I had learned or known about everything in the city. We were walking on streets where our ancestors had lived, and we toured every place mentioned in the bible. The visit to Yad Vashem was painful. I entered my dead brother's name among those of the others killed in the Shoah.

The next day, I was out at a restaurant and recognized my old friend Misi, one of the five twins from Budapest. He talked about our other friends in Israel: Harry Szusz was in the merchant navy and Pista was working for Paz gas company. When I asked Misi what he was doing, he replied that he worked for the government, but I felt he was hesitant to tell me more. He gave me Pista's telephone number. Later, when I met up with Pista, he told me that Misi was working for Shin Bet, the secret service. When we left Israel, we promised our friends that we would be back again soon.

A Promise of Light

Back in Toronto, our son Tov finished law school. He handed me his diploma and told me that he didn't want to be a lawyer and had only finished his courses because he knew I wanted him to finish what he started. He decided to go into the travel business, and he left for a Himalayan expedition with a new company that specialized in tourism to Thailand. He became a partner in the business and even learned to speak some Thai. He established and paid for several schools in Hill Tribe villages and encouraged tourists to donate to the schools as well.

Tov and his tour groups always spent some time in a village where he had a friendship with a young Thai lawyer whose father was chief of a Hill Tribe village. They treated Tov like their son. When Tov told them that he was getting married, they insisted he bring his bride, Lisa, and introduce her to them. They gave him a local wedding, including customary dress for him and for Lisa. Three neighbouring villages were invited for the festivities and the celebration lasted for three days.

When Tov and Lisa returned home, we made them get married under a chuppah, according to Jewish custom. We borrowed the chuppah from the Beth Tzedec synagogue and had our friend Rabbi Eddie Goldfarb officiate in Tov and Lisa's apartment. Our immediate family attended, and Lisa's parents later had a reception in Hamilton.

In the spring of 1983, our son Andrew was finishing medical

school and organizing his three months of clerking in a hospital. He announced that he wanted to spend those months in a hospital in Nepal because doctors were needed there and he could really help people. We were totally against it and tried to talk him out of it. We offered to pay his way to Israel, France or any western nation, but he wouldn't listen. To discourage him, I told him that I would not pay for his trip to Nepal. I don't know why, but I had a bad feeling about him going there. He made enough money to pay for his own trip.

At the end of June, he took off for his three months in Kathmandu, Nepal. On Yom Kippur morning, as the end of the three months neared and we were expecting his return, a police officer came to our door and told us that he was very sorry, but our son had died in Nepal. We could not believe it; we thought it must be a case of mistaken identity, that someone must have stolen his passport. We called an office in Ottawa, where they confirmed that it was true. He had died during the night of Kol Nidre. We were also told that in Nepal, they have no burials and instead, bodies are burned. The Nepalese people do not touch a dead body unless it is a family member, and then they wrap it in a white sheath, take it to the riverside and burn it. At that time, not a single body had been allowed out of the country. We could not accept this, and we insisted that we bring him back for a proper Jewish funeral. I demanded the Canadian government help us. We were told it was impossible, but that we should leave our number. Someone called back a few minutes later asking us to make out a cheque for five thousand dollars to the receiver general for future expenses, and they would do what they could.

My friend owned a travel agency and got us tickets for flights to India that same evening, and the following morning a flight from India to Nepal. Our friends brought food for us to take with us because we didn't have vaccinations and we planned not to eat any local foods. Our seats were on the plane's upper deck, and we were the only passengers until the plane landed in Amsterdam and about twenty yellow-robed monks came up to our compartment. One of the monks asked why we were seated there, since they had reserved the whole upper deck for the Dalai Lama. We explained our sad reason and said that the airline, as a courtesy, had given us the seats for privacy. A few minutes later, the Dalai Lama came over to us and said, "My secretary explained to me your sorrow. We believe in the afterlife, and your son will return as a holy man." He spoke perfect English, gave us an autographed book of his life story and blessed our journey. Although we did not believe in his religion, it did make us feel a little better.

In Delhi, India, a Canadian embassy member was waiting for us and drove us to a hotel. The next morning, we flew to Kathmandu. Again, a very professional Canadian diplomat waited for us. He took us to a hotel and left, saying he had a hundred things to do, that he had been told to do the impossible. Next we met Andrew's friends Mary and Ken, the secretary of CIDA, the Canadian International Development Agency. These two quiet, capable people sheltered us and guided us for the next thirty hours. And then it began. A wonderful procession of Andrew's friends and mentors at the hospital all came to be with us. Wendy from Virginia, Linda from New York, Lois from New Zealand and Tashi and her husband, Chris, from Australia, who looked so much like Andrew – tall, fair-hair, blue eyes. They all talked about how much they liked Andrew and how much they had learned from him about Judaism and medicine. Linda described his sympathy for the children in the hospital, how he held their hands and was there waiting when they came out of surgery.

First we went to Bir Hospital, where our son had spent his three months working, and met the heads of the hospital, Dr. Galong and Dr. Dixit. Dr. Dixit let us know that Andrew was an excellent doctor and that he himself had learned from him newer methods of doing stitches that did not leave such bad scars. Dr. Dixit told us that the medical students loved Andrew and that he had suggested they model themselves after Andrew and study what made him who he was. Dr. Galong told us how interesting it was speaking to Andrew about medicine, and how much our son knew. "I confess," he said, "that sometimes I told my colleagues I was busy with a procedure while Andy and I sat in my office drinking coffee and discussing medicine." Dr. Galong had never met a Jewish doctor before Andrew, and he had educated Dr. Galong about Judaism, especially how Jewish laws governed life, and how cleanliness was part of the religion.

Dr. Galong told us that apparently our son had died of dehydration due to diarrhea, and that he had not known Andrew was sick. He gave us a tour of the hospital. We noticed that there was no running water, very little medicine and even less nursing care. There were a lot of patients on stretchers in the hallways because there were not enough rooms.

The American embassy had provided one of the three spaces in their morgue, as well as a military coffin. We were grateful for their help. Canadian nurses had supervised the whole operation before we got there. They were sure, knowing Andrew, that we would be coming to get him. Next, we had to go to the British embassy to have afternoon tea with the ambassador and his wife. We tried to decline, but we were told it was a diplomatic necessity since Canada was a British Commonwealth country and they were representing us. They had our son's belongings, which they gave to us, and they were most gracious and helpful. They promised that their soldiers would take the casket to the airplane, if we were successful in getting permission from the Nepalese government to take him home. We had tea in the garden, served like I read about in British novels, with white-gloved waiters and silver trays. We could not enjoy it; our minds were not there.

We learned that our son had been in touch with the government because he wanted to go with a hired Sherpa guide into the mountain villages, where there were no doctors, to treat the sick. Andrew had collected a lot of medicines donated by the hospital and local pharmacists. He visited the government offices several times before they gave him permission. It was the Sherpa guide who had found his body.

Back in our hotel, our diplomat was waiting for us. He said it was a miracle, but all the people who helped us – including the Israelis, whom our Toronto friend Donald Carr called, the Americans, the British, and the hospital staff – had made the Nepalese government give in and allow Andrew to be taken out of Nepal to be buried in Canada.

I could not sleep all night. Early the next morning, looking out the window, I saw the mountains covered by mist. All of a sudden, the mist seemed to open and a white monastery appeared. The monastery stood out from the mist like a promise of light in the midst of darkness. I took it as a message that there was still hope for life. I woke up Ricky and we held on to each other, looking at the miracle.

At home, the funeral was emotional. Our good friends took care of everything that needed to be done. After the funeral, we received a call from an official in Ottawa asking our permission to allow him to publicize that it was the first time Canada had managed to get a dead body out of Nepal. Naturally, we declined. We did not want any publicity about our sorrow.

We established a fund at the university where our son had studied to help students wishing to do their clerking in a foreign country. With donations from us and a few friends, we also paid for an operating room in Bir Hospital in Kathmandu. Our son Tov visited the hospital once and noticed that Andrew's last name, engraved on the brass sign on the door, was unfortunately misspelled as "Masion."

Over the next couple of years, my wife had a hard time and could not accept the death of our son. She became ill and extremely depressed. The whole family tried to help her overcome her pain. She, too, tried very hard, but her grief was too much for her. She was taking too much aspirin, and one day when I got home from work, I found her sick. I got her to a hospital, but she had taken too many aspirins and passed away. In 1985, we buried her beside Andrew.

I was left alone and lonely. My children were wonderful and tried to keep me company, inviting me for dinner, but I did not want to become a burden to them. My friends also tried to include me in their lives. I knew that I wasn't good company, so I kept refusing most of the invitations. I put my mind and energy into my work. I couldn't live in the house alone, so I sold it and bought a condominium.

In 1986, I was fortunate to meet a wonderful woman named Doreen, who had lost her husband several years earlier. We had a lot in common and enjoyed each other's company. After a few months, I moved in with her and a year later, on March 7, 1987, we got married. Together we built a nice house on the shore of Lake Simcoe and spent a number of years enjoying the country life there. She is a warm-hearted person, and we built a new life together.

With Doreen's two children, Cheryl and Joel, and my three children, Robin, Tov and Roseanne, we had some wonderful Shabbat dinners. At the high holidays, we went to the Beth Tzedec cemetery to visit the graves of our spouses. To our surprise and shock we discovered that in that huge cemetery, where thousands of people are buried, our spouses were buried in the same row beside my son Andrew; only two spaces between them are open, which are for me and Doreen. Her husband died ten years prior to my wife. If I read this in a book, I would think it was the imagination of the writer. It is strange to think that when we die we will lie beside our first spouses, as well as our second. We think it must be fate. Doreen believes it was *bashert*, meant to be.

Life goes on and our children are married and all have children of their own – we now have thirteen grandchildren. I wonder if, subconsciously, I influenced my children to become what they are. Take Andrew, who died in Nepal – he was not interested in making money and wanted only to help people. Robin has a doctorate in psychology and works for the government in the health department in the area of violence against women. Tov continues with ecological tourism, and Roseanne worked in a synagogue helping families as a life cycle coordinator. Cheryl, Doreen's daughter, graduated in graphic design management and does work for the public schools. Doreen's son, Joel, is a medical doctor working as a clinician scientist at St. Michael's Hospital in Toronto.

Doreen and I were alone in our house and decided that we should take a long trip because for the first time, we had no responsibilities for the children. In 1991, Tov won plane tickets through Singapore Airlines at a travel agents' convention. He offered us the tickets as a present because he had been travelling enough and felt we would get more out of the trip. We gratefully accepted. It was an unbelievable trip and an unforgettable experience. We started with England, then went to Holland, and from there to India, Singapore and Indonesia. In Bali, a young monk drove us to a temple on top of a mountain. We were the only white tourists in the whole area. It was some kind of holiday, and the people were all dressed in yellow shirts. By coincidence, Doreen was also wearing yellow. We were not allowed into the temple during the services, but afterward, a priest came out and invited us in. We saw a huge altar covered with colourful fruits, and people bringing more in baskets on top on their heads. We were invited to join several families to eat and celebrate with them.

On the way back, we heard loud music near a park and saw a lot of people. We asked our driver what was going on and he told us it was a funeral. To us, it didn't look like a funeral. He parked the car and we walked over, and Doreen asked a man standing by to explain to us what was happening. The man said that a twenty-two-year-old had died in a motorcycle accident. The family had built a funeral tower and the body was lying on it. A few minutes later a procession marched to the tower and took the body, covered in a white shroud, to a wooden horse and placed the body inside. The priest poured gasoline on the body and set it on fire. In the meantime, music was playing and people were laughing and talking. It looked like more like a celebration than a funeral. The man explained that the youth was going to a better place, that the earth is only a stopping place before heaven.

We continued our sightseeing. I inquired as to whether there was a Jewish synagogue in the area. Our driver had no idea and didn't know what we meant by Jewish; he did not know anybody who was

Jewish. I wondered if I had found a place on this earth where there was no antisemitism. To me, it is an enigma that in all European countries there is antisemitism. We look the same, we abide by the laws of the countries where we live, we play the same sports, we go to the same schools. Why did so many in European countries help the Germans to kill Jews? I am trying to find a reason why some hate the Jewish people. In the various countries I travel, I ask the same questions. When I ask people the reason they hate Jews, most of the time they just look stunned and answer, "I don't know, I just hear that they cause trouble." Jews have been living in European countries for centuries as abiding citizens and hard workers, but the hate is passed on to the next generation.

While we were away, my father had a heart attack and was taken to hospital. When I went to visit he was alert, sitting up in bed. During our long visit, he asked me to explain how a fax machine worked. He said, "I cannot visualize how somebody can send me a letter from Hungary and minutes later I can read it." He passed away at ninety-three years old and he was true to himself until the end of his life. When he was ninety, he bought a piece of land on Hamilton Mountain and sold it for profit a year later. He was born in the horse-and-buggy age and died in the space age, when people landed on the moon. I miss him very much. May he rest in peace.

Eight years after his death, my mother passed away at the age of ninety-nine in the Shalom Village senior home in Hamilton. She was a remarkable, brave woman. In her youth, when girls were being married off by their parents, she refused. She selected her own husband, one whom she could love, and that she did. She adored my father. She was intelligent, resourceful and the best mother anybody could have.

⌒

Life was uneventful for a while, until one day we were invited to a dinner party where I met the president of the Toronto Holocaust Education Centre, Nate Leipciger, who happened to have been in

Mühldorf, the same camp I was in during the war. He is the only person I've met who was in that camp. I was glad to find out from him that the people who remained in camp after we left had survived. He talked me into becoming a speaker for the Holocaust organization. I hadn't spoken about the experience of the Holocaust to anyone, but he convinced me of the need to speak while we survivors were still alive.

In the late 1990s, my first speaking engagement was with high school students and their teachers on Holocaust Memorial Day. I was given one and a half hours to talk. I voiced my doubts that I could speak that long and was told a moderator would help me. To my surprise, I spoke for an hour and a half without stopping. Reflecting back, it was like opening a compressed container of my inner emotions. The words just poured out of me. The students were listening attentively, and they asked very intelligent questions. One said, "After what you went through, do you believe in God?" I gave an evasive answer.

Later, at home, I asked myself the same question. Having witnessed the murder of so many innocent people – young children, rabbis who had spent their whole lives studying and helping the poor – I could not believe there could be a God who would allow this to happen. I believe in tradition; I was born a Jew and will always be one. I try to live by the Jewish moral code and will live the rest of my life with those principles. I try to give to Jewish causes; I helped form the West Suburban Jewish Community Association; I belong to the Beth Tzedec Synagogue; and I go to high holiday services. But deep in my heart, I do not believe that there is a God who cares what I do, or what anybody does.

On the other hand, who or what created life? How did the order of the universe get created? I am not smart enough to answer these questions. Another student asked, "Has what happened to you changed the way you look at life?" I replied, "Definitely. First, I cannot see wasting food. It bothers me how much food goes to waste. I know that there is hunger everywhere and food can be hard to come by; the amount of food that goes into the garbage could feed a lot of hungry people. It also bothers me when people take their own lives. I think life is precious and we should live our lives the best way we can, while we can, and we should help those who need help. We don't know what life has in store for us. I believe in saving some money for retirement, but hoarding money and not enjoying life does not make sense to me." I told them that when I first got married, we saved one thousand dollars and I took my wife for a holiday. My father-in-law asked me how I could go and spend all my savings. I answered that money was to be spent and that when I came back, I would make more. He died young, only fifty-five years old, and never went farther than Barrie, Ontario.

I thought about how the Holocaust has affected my life. I don't want to be obsessed with my past, but everything has been somehow influenced by it and reminds me of what happened. When one of our children refused to eat some perfectly cooked food, I felt like saying, "In the camp..." and then I stopped and controlled my thoughts. I had made a decision that I would not raise our children with the trauma of the Holocaust. I did not speak to them about it until each reached the age of sixteen.

I continued to be a speaker to mainly non-Jewish students, and at churches and different organizations. One of the most rewarding experiences I had was when I was invited to speak to a Catholic school in Newmarket. Two Grade 8 classes came together in the biggest classroom and the students formed a semi-circle and listened to me speak. I started by asking them to imagine that what I experienced had happened to them, since I was exactly the same age at the time as they were. They listened for one hour without making a single noise. I finished by telling them that there are people who claim that the Holocaust never happened, and that now that they had heard me speak, they had all become witnesses and knew the Holocaust had happened.

The students all thanked me and lined up to take photos with me. Afterward, the teacher told me this had never happened before, that usually after the students listen to a speaker there is a mad rush out of the room. I believe that none of those students will ever become an antisemite. I could see the benefits of Holocaust education. The teacher told me that she was planning to go to Israel that summer and take a course at Yad Vashem to become a Holocaust educator.

I continued speaking for a few more years, but I had to stop because it was giving me sleepless nights, and when I did fall asleep, I had bad dreams. Doreen noticed that I was getting too involved and suggested that we take a trip. She wanted to go to Hungary. I remembered back to Ricky's same request and realized that the trip was not for me, but for Doreen. I reluctantly agreed, despite having said, after my last visit, that I would never go back. Doreen had always been interested in my stories of early childhood, especially the ones about my maternal grandmother's house in the village, where I used to spend summer holidays and my uncles took me fishing Friday afternoons to catch fish for Shabbat. I had told her about our winery and about our synagogue and mikvah in the backyard. My grandfather, who died before I was born, had built that synagogue. There wasn't any electricity in the village, only kerosene lamps. At noon, a drummer used to walk down the street yelling, "Hear it, hear it, this is the daily news."

Doreen suggested we take the trip while we were still physically able. I admitted that it was getting more tiring for me to travel. In May 2004, we planned the trip. I wanted to include a visit to Prague as well. We didn't need visas for Czechoslovakia or Hungary, but we needed one for Ukraine, where Bótrágy was now located. Doreen called the Ukrainian embassy for travel pamphlets and was told they didn't have any, nor did they have maps of Ukraine. She told them it was no wonder that people didn't want to go there.

In Prague, every tour operator featured the Jewish area as the number-one destination. We visited the famous cemetery where

Rabbi Loew was buried; according to legend, he built from clay the Golem who protected Jews in the city. There were six synagogues within five blocks, though only two synagogues still held services. One of them housed a number of Jewish ceremonial objects of great beauty. During the German occupation of Czechoslovakia the Nazis collected these objects, planning to show future generations how the now-extinct Jews had worshipped. We attended Friday night services at Altneu synagogue. Young Jewish men stood guard and checked passports before letting anybody in.

Doreen took a tour of the Theresienstadt ghetto and concentration camp. I could not go; mentally, I was not capable of seeing a concentration camp again. She was a bit depressed when she returned, but glad she went.

Next, we drove to Budapest, where we stayed in a new hotel beside the Danube River. By the Danube, a Holocaust memorial – sixty pairs of shoes cast in iron – commemorates all the Jews thrown in the river, murdered by the Hungarian Arrow Cross. We also visited the now completely restored Dohány synagogue. In my opinion, the Dohány is the most beautiful Reform synagogue in the world, but I could be biased. This time, I noticed a memorial plaque to Raoul Wallenberg on a wall. I was reading the information on the plaque as a film crew from Germany was taking a picture of it. They asked me if I knew who Wallenberg was and I mentioned that I had been the chairman for the Canadian Wallenberg organization. As I tried to educate them about Wallenberg's heroism in Hungary, they began interviewing me for the film. They knew a little of his story, but not the whole story. They were mainly interested in the way the Soviets treated diplomats after the war. I was glad that when they left they had a better understanding of what one man, a gentile, had done to save Jewish lives. At the back of the synagogue, we saw the memorial tree that had been erected with the support of the Jewish actor Tony Curtis. Every leaf bears the name of someone who died in the Shoah.

One thing I found upsetting was the resurgence of antisemitism in Hungary. A neo-Nazi party called Jobbik is exactly the image of the old Nazi party, openly asking to get the Jews out of Hungary. Six years after our trip, in the 2010 elections in Hungary, the Jobbik party won forty-seven seats in the parliament, which is about 16 per cent of the house. Ironically, one of the most antisemitic leaders of the Jobbik party, Csanád Szegedi, who had been raised as a gentile, turned out to have a Jewish background. Apparently, in 2012, his grandmother told him that she was a Holocaust survivor. He resigned from the party. I heard that he began taking lessons from a rabbi.

We spent more time visiting the Jewish areas of the city. To my surprise, many storefronts still had Hebrew lettering. Although there is an active Jewish presence in Budapest, I'm very wary of it. If the Jewish population would listen to me, I'd advise them to make plans to leave the country.

We drove to Újhely, where I knew there was a border crossing to Ukraine. At the border, we were stopped by Ukrainian guards with machine guns. They took our passports and disappeared for half an hour. One of them returned our passports and said "Nyet," which I knew meant no. He didn't speak any English or Hungarian, so we had no choice but to turn back. We tried another crossing I knew of about thirty kilometres away, but the same thing happened. This time, a Hungarian man there told me that we could have gone across without our car, which did not have the proper papers; the concern was that we could sell the car for a profit in Ukraine. He advised us to go to a nearby village and find the taxi driver who lived next to the church. The taxi driver's car was broken but he suggested we go a tavern twenty kilometres away to get someone to take us over the border. We located the tavern, spoke to the owner, and shortly after, an old car appeared with two young men in it.

We made arrangements with them to take us into Ukraine and left our rental car, with *all* our belongings, with the tavern owner. We got in the old car and went over a wooden bridge to the border on the other side. After a lengthy delay at the border station, where our driver was questioned, we finally started off to my grandmother's house in Bótrágy. We hadn't driven more than two kilometres when a Ukrainian police car pulled us over. Our driver opened his window and, without a word, handed over some money. The policeman took it, saluted and drove away. Our driver then asked us if we minded if he stopped to buy some gasoline. He drove up to an old gas pump and proceeded to put a railway tie under the car. He then tilted the car so he could put in more gasoline, and filled two empty tanks as well, which he put in the trunk to take back to Hungary. Gas was much cheaper in Ukraine.

A short time later, we were driving around the village of Bótrágy, looking for my grandmother's house. I couldn't find it, so we asked around, but no one could help us. I tried to locate the house by going in the approximate direction of the Jewish cemetery, but it was difficult to find. There weren't any Jews left in the village, so the cemetery was never used. The only thing left near there was a wire gate with a Magen David on it. All the stones were gone. People had taken them and used them as steps in front of their houses.

We continued driving and found a non-Jewish cemetery, where a couple of women were working. I inquired who the oldest person in the village was, hoping that person might know where my grandmother's house was. They answered, "Elsa," and pointed to where she happened to be, right nearby, walking with the support of two other women. Elsa looked about one hundred years old. She said, "I knew your grandmother; everybody loved her." Elsa had worked for my grandmother, helping on Shabbat. She pointed down the road and told us the house was on the end of it, at the corner. Now, I recognized the corner, but not the house. Elsa explained that the government had torn the house down and sold the lot for back taxes; there were now two houses on the lot. The synagogue and mikvah were also gone, but the out buildings in the backyard were still there.

I had had enough. I felt upset about my past and my memories and I was ready to leave. However, when our driver asked if he could stop for a short visit with a couple of friends, I didn't mind. We talked with them briefly. As we were leaving, one friend gave our driver a few cartons of cigarettes, which he stashed under the dashboard. He was taking them back to Hungary as cigarettes were also much cheaper in Ukraine. We got back to the tavern without any problems, saw that our car and its contents were intact, and paid the drivers a reasonable price (which was suggested by the woman at the tavern, since none of us knew what to charge). The drivers had had a good day – they got gasoline and cigarettes and made some money. They were so pleased that they insisted on treating us to drinks.

We drove back to Budapest and spent more time exploring the renewed Jewish life of the city. We visited Kazinczy street, with its Jewish antique stores, and bought an old Chanukah candelabra made from brass. It came apart into several pieces; we were told it was over one hundred years old. We visited the synagogue on the street where I used to go for Shabbat services. I showed Doreen where I had gotten together with my friends to eat chestnut purée. All of a sudden, my mind turned to all the people who had died in my family. I told Doreen that I'd had enough of memories and wanted to get back to our present life. Besides some pleasant childhood memories, there were too many bad ones. We flew home saddened for the past, thinking about how hard it is to go back.

~

In 2010, we decided to take another trip overseas. I'd been interested in the arts my whole life and had seen great masters' works in various museums. The Hermitage in St. Petersburg had always been a collection I hoped to see. The opportunity arose when we saw an ad for a cruise to St. Petersburg. We liked the itinerary aside from a stop in Germany. I was reluctant to go to Germany because I thought it would be too traumatic for me. I really didn't want to stop there, but I couldn't change the plan. The organizers told me that there was a tour of Jewish sites in Berlin, so I agreed to go.

We embarked in Copenhagen, Denmark, and stopped at Warne-münde, two hundred kilometres outside of Berlin. We took a private car into Berlin for two days and hired a local guide for the Jewish tour. We visited the Jewish museum, the Holocaust memorial, sites of old synagogues, the book-burning place and the Berlin Wall. On the way back in the car, I was sitting beside the driver, a German man about thirty-five years old. He was talking on his cellphone in German. I understood what he was saying and made a remark because it concerned us. He looked at me, surprised that I could speak the language, and then asked, "Can you explain something that has been bothering me? How could the Germans pick out who was Jewish? I am looking at you and I cannot tell any difference between you or anybody else." I explained that before the war, people had to fill in a census, registering the religion they followed, as well as where they worked and lived. The government knew every Jewish person's name and there was no place for them to escape. Jews had lived in Germany all their lives, for generations, and they were Germans, integrated into society. Judaism was their religion, but they were German citizens. I could not get over how I felt about what these people had done to us. How could the people who had created all the beauty and advancement in this city have produced so many people willing to help murder millions of innocents? I was glad to leave.

Our next stop was St. Petersburg, where we also hired a private tour guide. We asked her to take us to the synagogue. It was a Tuesday morning at ten o'clock and the synagogue was near empty. Doreen went upstairs to see the women's section and I, not wanting to stand alone, walked over to the three men who were there. One of them had a beard, so I figured he must be the rabbi. Another asked me what had brought me there. I mentioned the cruise and that we had just come from Berlin. The taller gentleman asked, "And how did you like Berlin?" I replied, "I am the wrong person to ask because I hate that country and I hate those people." He answered by saying, "Let me introduce myself. I am the secretary of the foreign office of Germany and this other gentleman is in charge of Jewish affairs in Berlin." I replied, "I'm not going to apologize. The Germans killed most of my family and I was taken to Auschwitz at the age of fifteen." He responded that there was no need to apologize, that he understood how I must have felt in Berlin. "But let me tell you about the new Germany. We have more than 50,000 Jews living in Berlin. We have the strongest laws against antisemitism, and we teach our children that the Nazis murdered – not killed, murdered – the European Jewish populations. We have put signs in front of every apartment building where Jewish people were murdered. Denying the Holocaust is a crime in Germany." He reached into his wallet, gave me his card and said that if he could do anything for me, to give him a call. The card said Dr. Wolf-Ruthart Born, State Secretary, Federal Foreign Office. I left there with mixed emotions. Should we hate Germans for their fathers' sins? I recalled my conversation with the German driver. I could see that the education of the German youth was not as complete as the secretary of the foreign office thought it was. We continued our tour to the Scandinavian nations, but I could not forget the bitter taste of my experience in Germany.

Epilogue

The 1,000 orphans who were brought to Canada in 1948 did remarkably well. I don't know if the government conducted a survey, but what I do know is that among those in Hamilton, my friend Zoltan Freeman became part-owner of a chocolate factory, and eventually owned the whole factory. Upon selling it, he helped establish a Holocaust centre in Winnipeg. He was known as a philanthropist and helped several good causes. My brother Fredi became president of automotive parts for Best Buy and was named best businessman for many years. He was also part-owner of two wholesale auto parts stores. Two of our boys, Morris and Dugyu, owned and operated a kitchen remodelling and flooring business. I know that elsewhere, some orphans became doctors, others professors, lawyers and developers. I had a successful denture clinic and was involved in land development. I am now retired and enjoying my time with our grandchildren. I've made some jewellery and have made lots of miniature sculptures from gold representing different Judaica symbols such as a menorah, a Torah and a bride and groom under the chuppah. I also did some stone sculpting. One piece of soapstone I started to shape subconsciously turned into a clenched fist. To me it symbolically represented "Never Again."

We all thank Canada, the best country in the world, for giving us these opportunities. Canada has opened its doors to those in need from all over the world – people of every nationality and religion. Perhaps the greatest insight that I can share, as a Canadian Jew who wandered through a pit of inhuman hell and then surfaced in this most beautiful country, is that if the rest of the world would follow Canada, where people live peacefully with one another, the world would be a much better place for all. I read in the newspaper that in Hungary, Sweden and other countries, antisemitism has reared its ugly head once more and, with it, a hate of so many others beyond the few Jews who now live there. It is sadly ironic that Muslims, too, have become a centrepoint of European hatred, at a time in history when many have cast doubt on the historical legitimacy of Israel as a Jewish state and a symbol of hope for fair leadership in the Middle East and beyond. Can the world learn from its past? I believe that it can.

I finished writing my memoirs in my eighty-second year of life. When I was in the Nazi camps, I was only fifteen years old. I am part of those who are called "child survivors," but at that time of my life I was partly a child, partly a young adult. My emotional thinking while I was writing was influenced by time. The way I felt emotionally in the camp, I could not put down on paper. At that age I still wanted my mother, but at the same time, I realized the reality of the situation. The loneliness and fear are difficult to recreate.

Had I been a couple of years younger or older, I probably would not have survived. For example, a couple of years older, I don't think the German soldier would have told me to go to work that day. A couple of years younger, I would not have gotten past the selections in Auschwitz. While I was a speaker for the Holocaust Centre, the most common question was, "What do you consider the reason for your survival, when so many people around you died?" I was never able to give a concrete answer when I asked myself the same question. I try to put together all the situations when my life was in imminent danger, and I come to the conclusion that it was partly luck, as well as the ability to adapt to changing situations.

When I started this story of my life, I was not trying to write a literary masterpiece, only an eyewitness account of the happenings that I saw or was personally involved in. Even today, while survivors are still alive, there are people denying that the Holocaust happened. In the long memory of history, some major events receive only a footnote. But the magnitude of the systematic, pre-planned murder of six million Jewish people is unique and unequalled in history. The German people will have to carry the burden that their ancestors were guilty of initiating this human tragedy.

Glossary

aliyah (Hebrew; pl. *aliyot*, literally, ascent) A term used by Jews and modern Israelis to refer to Jewish immigration to Israel; the term is also used to refer to "going up" to the altar in a synagogue to read from the Torah.

American Jewish Joint Distribution Committee (JDC) Also known colloquially as the "Joint." A charitable organization founded in 1914 to provide humanitarian assistance and relief to Jews all over the world in times of crisis. It provided material support for persecuted Jews in Germany and other Nazi-occupied territories and facilitated their immigration to neutral countries such as Portugal, Turkey and China. Between 1939 and 1944, JDC officials helped close to 81,000 European Jews find asylum in various parts of the world. Between 1944 and 1947, the JDC assisted more than 100,000 refugees living in DP camps by offering retraining programs, cultural activities and financial assistance for emigration.

Anger, Per (1913–2002) Second secretary of the Swedish legation in Budapest, Hungary, from 1942 to 1945. Anger originated the idea of providing provisional passports to Hungarian Jews in an effort to save their lives. He worked with Raoul Wallenberg in rescue efforts and, after the end of World War II, worked to uncover Wallenberg's fate. He was awarded the title of Righteous Among the Nations by Yad Vashem in 1982. *See also* Wallenberg, Raoul; Yad Vashem.

antisemitism Prejudice, discrimination, persecution and/or hatred against Jewish people, institutions, culture and symbols.

Arrow Cross Party (in Hungarian, Nyilaskeresztes Párt – Hungarista Mozgalom; abbreviation: Nyilas) A Hungarian nationalistic and antisemitic party founded by Ferenc Szálasi in 1935 under the name the Party of National Will. With the full support of Nazi Germany, the newly renamed Arrow Cross Party ran in Hungary's 1939 election and won 25 per cent of the vote. The party was banned shortly after the elections, but was legalized again in March 1944 when Germany occupied Hungary. Under Nazi approval, the party assumed control of Hungary from October 15, 1944, to March 1945, led by Szálasi under the name the Government of National Unity. The Arrow Cross regime was particularly brutal toward Jews – in addition to the thousands of Hungarian Jews who had been deported to Nazi death camps during the previous Miklós Horthy regime, the Arrow Cross, during their short period of rule, instigated the murder of tens of thousands of Hungarian Jews. In one specific incident on November 8, 1944, more than 70,000 Jews were rounded up and sent on a death march to Nazi camps in Austria. Between December 1944 and January 1945, the Arrow Cross murdered approximately 20,000 Jews, many of whom had been forced into a closed ghetto at the end of November 1944.

Auschwitz (German; in Polish, Oświęcim) A town in southern Poland approximately forty kilometres from Krakow, it is also the name of the largest complex of Nazi concentration camps, which were built nearby. The Auschwitz complex contained three main camps: Auschwitz I, a slave labour camp built in May 1940; Auschwitz II-Birkenau, a death camp built in early 1942; and Auschwitz-Monowitz, a slave labour camp built in October 1942. In 1941, Auschwitz I was a testing site for usage of the lethal gas Zyklon B as a method of mass killing, which then went into wide usage. Between 1942 and 1944, transports arrived at Auschwitz-

Birkenau from almost every country in Europe – hundreds of thousands from both Poland and Hungary, and thousands from France, the Netherlands, Greece, Slovakia, Bohemia and Moravia, Yugoslavia, Belgium, Italy and Norway. Between May 15 and July 8, 1944, approximately 435,000 Hungarian Jews were deported to Auschwitz. As well, more than 30,000 people were deported there from other concentration camps. It is estimated that 1.1 million people were murdered in Auschwitz; approximately 950,000 were Jewish; 74,000 Polish; 21,000 Roma; 15,000 Soviet prisoners of war; and 10,000–15,000 other nationalities. The Auschwitz complex was liberated by the Soviet army in January 1945.

bar mitzvah, bat mitzvah (Hebrew; literally, son/daughter of the commandment) The time when, in Jewish tradition, children become religiously and morally responsible for their actions and are considered adults for the purpose of synagogue and other rituals. Traditionally this occurs at age thirteen for boys and twelve for girls. Historically, girls were not included in this ritual until the latter half of the twentieth century, when liberal Jews instituted an equivalent ceremony and celebration for girls called a bat mitzvah. A bar/bat mitzvah marks the attainment of adulthood by a ceremony during which the boy/girl is called upon to read a portion of the Torah and recite the prescribed prayers in a public prayer service.

Blum, André Léon (1872–1950) Prime minister of France from June 4, 1936, to June 22, 1937, and March 13, 1938, to April 10, 1938; and president of the provisional government of the French Republic from December 16, 1946, to January 22, 1947. After the German occupation of France in June 1940, Blum was arrested for treason and in 1943 he was deported to the Buchenwald concentration camp. He was sent to Dachau concentration camp in April 1945 and then transferred to German-occupied South Tyrol in Italy, where he was liberated in May 1945.

Born, Wolf-Ruthart (1944–) A German diplomat who served as

State Secretary of the Federal Foreign Office in Berlin from 2009 to 2011.

Canadian Jewish Congress (CJC) An advocacy organization and lobbying group for the Canadian Jewish community from 1919 to 2011. In 1947, the CJC convinced the Canadian government to re-issue Privy Council Order 1647 – originally adopted in 1942 to admit five hundred Jewish refugee children from Vichy France, although they never made it out – that allowed for one thousand Jewish children under the age of eighteen to be admitted to Canada. Under the auspices of the CJC, who would provide for the refugees' care, the War Orphans Project was established in April 1947 and the CJC began searching for Jewish war orphans with the help of the United Nations Relief and Rehabilitation Administration (UNRRA). Between 1947 and 1949, 1,123 young Jewish refugees came to Canada. The CJC was restructured in 2007 and its functions subsumed under the Centre for Israel and Jewish Affairs (CIJA) in 2011.

Chanukah (also Hanukah; Hebrew; dedication) An eight-day festival celebrated in December to mark the victory of the Jews against foreign conquerors who desecrated the Temple in Jerusalem in the second century BCE. Traditionally, each night of the festival is marked by lighting an eight-branch candelabrum called a menorah to commemorate the rededication of the Temple and the miracle of its lamp burning for eight days without oil.

cheder (Hebrew; literally, room) An Orthodox Jewish elementary school that teaches the fundamentals of Jewish religious observance and textual study, as well as the Hebrew language.

cholent (Yiddish) A traditional Jewish slow-cooked pot stew usually eaten as the main course at the festive Shabbat lunch on Saturdays after the synagogue service and on other Jewish holidays. For Jews of Eastern-European descent, the basic ingredients of *cholent* are meat, potatoes, beans and barley.

chuppah (Hebrew; literally, covering) The canopy used in traditional Jewish weddings that is usually made of a cloth (sometimes a prayer shawl) stretched or supported over four poles. It is meant to symbolize the home the couple will build together.

Communist Party of Hungary First founded in 1918 and resurrected in 1945 following the liberation and occupation of Hungary by the Soviet Union. The Party was assisted both openly and clandestinely by the USSR and initially had the support of many Hungarians who had opposed the wartime pro-Nazi government in Hungary. The Communist Party merged with the Social Democratic Party in 1948 and was renamed the Hungarian Working People's Party and then, in 1956, the Hungarian Socialist Workers' Party; it consolidated total power in Hungary by 1949, which it held until 1989.

Czech Family Camp (Auschwitz) A section of the Birkenau "quarantine" camp, where recent arrivals were housed temporarily, that was reserved for the more than 10,000 Czech Jewish prisoners who were deported from the Theresienstadt camp between September and December 1943. For approximately six months, the Czech Jews were accorded privileges such as receiving parcels and writing letters in an effort to counteract rumours that the Nazis were annihilating Jews, but they were eventually subjected to the same fate as other prisoners at Birkenau. Thousands were murdered in the gas chambers on March 8 and 9, 1944; a few months later, in July, after a selection that found only a few thousand fit for forced labour, the rest of the family camp, more than seven thousand Czech Jews, were sent to the gas chambers. *See also* Auschwitz; Theresienstadt.

DP camps Facilities set up by the Allied authorities and the United Nations Relief and Rehabilitation Administration (UNRRA) in October 1945 to resolve the refugee crisis that arose at the end of World War II. The camps provided temporary shelter and assistance to the millions of people – not only Jews – who had been displaced from their home countries as a result of the war and helped them prepare for resettlement. *See also* Feldafing.

Eichmann, Adolf (1906–1962) The head of the Gestapo department responsible for the implementation of the Nazis' policy of mass murder of Jews (the so-called Final Solution), Eichmann was in charge of transporting Jews to death camps in Poland. In 1942, Eichmann coordinated deportations of Jewish populations from Slovakia, the Netherlands, France and Belgium. In 1944, he was directly involved in the deportations of Jews from Hungary, as well as in negotiations with Rudolf Kasztner to supply Jews for slave labour in Austria. After the war, Eichmann escaped from US custody and fled to Argentina, where he was captured in 1960 by Israeli intelligence operatives; his ensuing 1961 trial in Israel was widely and internationally televised. Eichmann was sentenced to death and hanged in May 1962. *See also* Hausner, Gideon.

Feldafing The first DP camp for Jewish survivors of the Holocaust, opened in May 1945. Located thirty kilometres southwest of Munich, it had previously been a Hitlerjugend (Hitler Youth) summer camp. In the DP camp, religious and secular schools were established for children, and an evening school and a vocational training school were created for adults. There was also a rich cultural life, with newspapers, a theatre troupe and an orchestra organized by camp residents. The camp was closed in 1953. *See also* DP camps; Hitlerjugend.

ghetto A confined residential area for Jews. The term originated in Venice, Italy, in 1516 with a law requiring all Jews to live on a segregated, gated island known as Ghetto Nuovo. Throughout the Middle Ages in Europe, Jews were often forcibly confined to gated Jewish neighbourhoods. During the Holocaust, the Nazis forced Jews to live in crowded and unsanitary conditions in rundown districts of cities and towns.

Habonim (Hebrew; literally, builders) A Labour Zionist group that encouraged Jewish youth to become pioneers in Palestine and help build the Jewish homeland. It promoted activities such as camping and scouting, and educated youth in Jewish history. Labour Zionism is a secular socialist Zionist movement that promotes the building of a Jewish state through the efforts of Jewish workers. *See also* Zionism.

Hasidic Judaism (from the Hebrew word *hasid*; literally, piety) An Orthodox Jewish spiritual movement founded by Rabbi Israel ben Eliezer in eighteenth-century Poland; characterized by philosophies of mysticism and focusing on joyful prayer. This movement resulted in a new kind of leader who attracted disciples as opposed to the traditional rabbis who focused on the intellectual study of Jewish law. Melody and dance have an important role in Hasidic worship. There are many different sects of Hasidic Judaism, but followers of Hasidism often wear dark, conservative clothes as well as a head covering to reflect modesty and show respect to God.

Hausner, Gideon (1915–1990) An Israeli lawyer and politician. As Attorney General of Israel, Hausner led the legal team that prosecuted Adolf Eichmann for war crimes in Jerusalem in 1961. He also served in the Knesset and as council chairman of Yad Vashem. *See also* Eichmann, Adolf; Yad Vashem.

Hitlerjugend (German) Known in English as the Hitler Youth, Hitlerjugend (HJ) was founded in 1926. By 1935, 60 per cent of the German youth – boys and girls – were members of the HJ and on December 1, 1936, all other youth groups were banned. In 1939, HJ membership was made compulsory for youths over seventeen, after which membership comprised 90 per cent of German youth. The focus of the paramilitary organization was to create soldiers for the Third Reich who were properly indoctrinated in Nazi ideology. The girls' branch of the HJ was the Bund Deutscher Mädel (BDM).

Horthy, Miklós (1868–1957) The regent of Hungary during the interwar period and for much of World War II. Horthy presided over a government that was aligned with the Axis powers and supported Nazi ideology. After the German army occupied Hungary in

March 1944, Horthy served primarily as a figurehead to the pro-
Nazi government; nevertheless, he was able to order the suspen-
sion of the deportation of Hungarian Jews to death camps in the
beginning of July 1944. Horthy planned to withdraw his country
from the war on October 15, 1944, but the Nazis supported an Arrow Cross coup that same day and forced Horthy to abdicate.

Iron Curtain A term coined by Sir Winston Churchill in 1946 to de-
scribe the metaphorical boundary that physically and ideologi-
cally divided Europe into two separate spheres of influence at the
end of World War II: one in Eastern Europe, controlled politically,
militarily and economically by the Soviet Union; the second in
Western Europe, allied with Western liberal democracies, economically predisposed to market economics and under the military protection of the United States.

Jewish Agency A non-governmental organization that assists Jews
in settling and developing the land of Israel. It was established in
1929 under the League of Nations' Mandate for Palestine.

Jobbik (Hungarian; abbreviation of Jobbik Magyarországért Mozgalom, meaning Movement for a Better Hungary) A radical, conservative political party in Hungary that supports nationalistic policies against foreign, especially Jewish, investment and has been
linked to attacks against Jewish and Romani Hungarians. The Jobbik party's influence in Hungarian politics has been growing since
its inception in 2003; in the 2010 elections, it won 16.7 per cent of
the seats in the Hungarian National Assembly, and in 2014, it won
20.3 per cent of seats.

Kaddish (Aramaic; holy) Also known as the Mourner's Prayer, Kaddish is said as part of mourning rituals in Jewish prayer services
as well as at funerals and memorials. Sons are required to say
Kaddish daily for eleven months after the death of a parent and
also each year, on the anniversary of the death. The word Kaddish
comes from a Hebrew root word meaning "holy."

kapo (German) A concentration camp prisoner appointed by the SS to oversee other prisoners as slave labourers.

kibbutz (Hebrew) A collectively owned farm or settlement in Israel, democratically governed by its members.

kippah Small head covering worn by Jewish men as a sign of reverence for God.

Labour Service (in Hungarian, *Munkaszolgálat*) Hungary's military-related labour service system, which was first established in 1919 for those considered too "politically unreliable" for regular military service. After the labour service was made compulsory in 1939, Jewish men of military age were recruited to serve; however, having been deemed "unfit" to bear arms, they were equipped with tools and employed in mining, road and rail construction and maintenance work. Though the men were treated relatively well at first, the system became increasingly punitive in nature. By 1941, Jews in forced labour battalions were required to wear a yellow armband and civilian clothes; they had no formal rank and were unarmed; they were often mistreated by extremely antisemitic supervisors; and their work included clearing minefields, causing their death. Between 20,000 and 40,000 Jewish men died during their forced labour service.

Loew, Rabbi Judah (1520–1609) Known as Judah Loew ben Bezalel, and also as the Maharal (a Hebrew acronym that translates to our teacher, Rabbi Loew) of Prague, Loew was a prominent Talmudic scholar, mystic and philosopher. It is claimed that Loew created a Golem, a being of clay, to protect and defend the Jews of Prague from antisemitic attacks. Loew led congregations in the cities of both Mikulov and Prague.

mikvah (Hebrew; literally, a pool or gathering of water) A ritual purification bath taken by Jews on occasions that denote change, such as before the Sabbath (signifying the shift from a regular weekday to a holy day of rest), as well as those that denote a change in personal status, such as before a person's wedding or, for a married woman, after menstruation. The word mikvah refers to both the pool of water and the building that houses the ritual bath.

Mühldorf A complex of four subcamps, one of which was Waldlager, established in Bavaria by the SS in the middle of 1944. Under the supervision of Organisation Todt, subterranean factories for the production of aircraft and weapons were constructed by the more than 8,000 prisoners who were held there. An estimated 2,200 to 3,900 people were killed in the Mühldorf camps – from abuse, overwork and disease. SS guards sent about 3,600 prisoners on death marches from the camp in April 1945 in an attempt to evade the approaching US army. How many survived is unknown. *See also* Organisation Todt, Waldlager.

Organisation Todt A construction and civil engineering group named for its founder, Fritz Todt, that undertook major civilian and military projects under the Nazis. It began as a quasi-governmental agency but in 1942 it was absorbed by the German government, becoming part of the Ministry of Armaments and War Production under Albert Speer. The Todt organization made extensive use of forced and slave labour during the war.

Orthodox Judaism The set of beliefs and practices of Jews for whom the observance of Jewish law is closely connected to faith; it is characterized by strict religious observance of Jewish dietary laws, restrictions on work on the Sabbath and holidays, and a code of modesty in dress.

Palestine The area of the Middle East under British rule from 1923 to 1948, as established by the League of Nations after World War I. During that time, the United Kingdom severely restricted Jewish immigration. The Mandate area encompassed present-day Israel, Jordan, the West Bank and the Gaza Strip.

pogrom (Russian; to wreak havoc, to demolish) A violent attack on a distinct ethnic group. The term most commonly refers to nineteenth- and twentieth-century attacks on Jews in the Russian Empire.

Purim (Hebrew; literally, lots) The celebration of the Jews' escape from annihilation in Persia. The Purim story, as described in the biblical Book of Esther, recounts how Haman, advisor to the King of Persia, planned to rid Persia of Jews, and how Queen Esther and her cousin Mordecai foiled Haman's plot by convincing the king to save the Jews. During the Purim festivities, people dress up as one of the figures in the Purim story, hold parades and retell the story of Haman, Esther and Mordecai.

Rákosi, Mátyás (1892–1971) The Hungarian dictator who led the country as General Secretary of the Hungarian Communist Party from 1945 to 1956.

Roma Also known as Romani. An ethnic group primarily located in central and eastern Europe. The Roma were commonly referred to as Gypsies in the past, a term now generally considered to be derogatory, and they have often lived on the fringes of society and been subject to persecution. During the Holocaust, which the Roma refer to in Romani as the *Porajmos* – the devouring – they were stripped of their citizenship under the Nuremberg Laws and were targeted for death under Hitler's race policies. At Auschwitz-Birkenau, a separate camp was set up for the Roma, where they were subjected to brutal treatment, starvation, medical experiments and murder in the gas chambers. The Roma Family Camp was liquidated on August 2, 1944. The estimation of how many Roma were killed varies widely and has been difficult to document – estimates generally range between 200,000 and one million.

Schutzpass (German; pl. *Schutzpässe*; protective pass) A visa that identified the holder as a Swedish subject. Swedish diplomat Raoul Wallenberg issued these passes to at least 15,000 Hungarian Jews, thereby saving them from deportation. See also Wallenberg, Raoul.

Shabbat (Hebrew; Sabbath) The weekly day of rest beginning Friday at sunset and ending Saturday at nightfall, ushered in by the lighting of candles on Friday evening and the recitation of blessings over wine and challah (braided egg bread); a day of celebration as well as prayer, it is customary to eat three festive meals, attend synagogue services and refrain from doing any work or travelling.

Shabbat goy A non-Jewish person who performs tasks that are religiously forbidden to Jews on the Sabbath.

simcha (Hebrew; gladness, joy) Generally refers to a festive occasion.

SS *St. Louis* An ocean liner that sailed from Hamburg, Germany, on May 13, 1939, with 937 passengers on board, most of them German Jewish refugees fleeing the Nazis. Their destination was Cuba, where they sought temporary refuge before being admitted into the United States. Both countries, however, refused entry to the passengers – as did Canada – and the ship was forced to return to Europe, eventually docking in Belgium. Passengers were given refuge in Britain, France, Belgium and Holland, but after the May 1940 Nazi invasion of France and the Low Countries, the passengers were once again targets of Nazi persecution. It is estimated that approximately 250 perished in the Holocaust.

Stalin, Joseph (1878–1953) The leader of the Soviet Union from 1924 until his death in 1953. After acquiring leadership of the Communist Party, Stalin ousted rivals, killed opponents in purges, and effectively established himself as a dictator. During the war and in the immediate post-war period, many Jews in Poland viewed Stalin as the leader of the country that liberated them and saved them from death at the hands of the Nazis, unaware of the extent of Stalin's own murderous policies. Stalin was brutal toward Soviet prisoners of war, considering them "traitors" and refusing to sign the Geneva Convention, which would likely have assured them better treatment. Instead, thousands died in captivity in Germany. After World War II, Stalin set up Communist governments controlled by Moscow in many Eastern European states bordering and close to the USSR, and instituted antisemitic campaigns and purges.

Star of David (in Hebrew, *Magen David*) The six-pointed star that is the ancient and most recognizable symbol of Judaism. During World War II, Jews in Nazi-occupied areas were frequently forced to wear a badge or armband with the Star of David on it as an identifying mark of their lesser status and to single them out as targets for persecution.

tefillin (Hebrew) Phylacteries. A pair of black leather boxes containing scrolls of parchment inscribed with Bible verses and worn by Jews on the arm and forehead at prescribed times of prayer as a symbol of the covenantal relationship with God. Some synagogues have Tefillin Clubs, social groups at which men and boys past bar-mitzvah age are encouraged to put on *tefillin* and learn about their Jewish heritage.

Theresienstadt A walled town in the Czech Republic sixty kilometres north of Prague that served as both a ghetto and a concentration camp. More than 73,000 Jews from the German Protectorate of Bohemia and Moravia and from the Greater German Reich (including Austria and parts of Poland) were deported to Terezin between 1941 and 1945, 60,000 of whom were deported to Auschwitz or other death camps. Terezin was showcased as a "model" ghetto for propaganda purposes to demonstrate to delegates from the International Red Cross and others the "humane" treatment of Jews and to counter information reaching the Allies about Nazi atrocities and mass murder. Theresienstadt was liberated on May 8, 1945, by the Soviet Red Army.

Treaty of Trianon One of the five treaties produced at the 1919 Paris Peace Conference organized by the victors of World War I. The Treaty of Trianon imposed a harsh peace on Hungary, exacting reparations and redrawing its borders so that Hungary lost over two-thirds of its territory and about two-thirds of its inhabitants.

Waldlager (German; literally, forest camp) A part of the Mühldorf camp complex in Bavaria. About 2,250 male and female prisoners were held there, living in tents or in earth huts, of which only the roofs were visible above ground. Most of the prisoners were Hungarian Jews, who were forced to do heavy construction work. *See also* Mühldorf.

Wallenberg, Raoul (1912–1947?) The Swedish diplomat who was sent to Hungary in June 1944 by the US Refugee Board and succeeded in saving tens of thousands of Budapest Jews by issuing them Swedish certificates of protection or *Schutzpässe*. The Swedish government also authorized Wallenberg to set up thirty "safe houses" and organize food distribution, medical assistance and child care for Jews in Budapest. Of the slightly more than 100,000 Jews that remained alive in Budapest at the end of the war (out of a pre-war population of 247,000), the majority were saved through his efforts. Wallenberg was arrested by the Soviets in 1945; his fate remains unknown. He was awarded the title of Righteous Among the Nations by Yad Vashem in 1986 and has been honoured by memorials or monuments in ten other countries. *See also* Schutz-pass.

wood gas A synthetic gas fuel used as an alternative to gasoline in furnaces, stoves and vehicles. It is made through a process of gas-ifying wood or other carbon-based materials to produce carbon monoxide and hydrogen, which can then be used as fuel.

Yad Vashem The Holocaust Martyrs' and Heroes' Remembrance Authority, established in 1953 to commemorate, educate the public about, research and document the Holocaust.

Yiddish A language derived from Middle High German with elements of Hebrew, Aramaic, Romance and Slavic languages, and written in Hebrew characters. Spoken by Jews in east-central Europe for roughly a thousand years from the tenth century to the mid-twentieth century, it was still the most common language among European Jews until the outbreak of World War II. There are similarities between Yiddish and contemporary German.

Yom Kippur (Hebrew; literally, day of atonement) A solemn day of fasting and repentance that comes eight days after Rosh Hashanah, the Jewish New Year, and marks the end of the high holidays.

Zionism A movement promoted by the Viennese Jewish journalist Theodor Herzl, who argued in his 1896 book *Der Judenstaat* (The Jewish State) that the best way to resolve the problem of antisemitism and persecution of Jews in Europe was to create an independent Jewish state in the historic Jewish homeland of Biblical Israel. Zionists also promoted the revival of Hebrew as a Jewish national language.

Photographs

1

2

1 & 2 Adolf and Esther Friedman, Michael's paternal grandparents. Date unknown.

Michael's parents, Gisel (née Weisz) and Ferencz Friedman. Beregszász, circa
1923.

1

2

1 The Friedman family before the war. Left to right: Michael's older brother, Laci; his mother, Gisel; his sister, Magda; his father, Ferencz; and Michael. In front: Michael's younger brother, Fredi. Újhely, circa 1936.

2 Michael with his family after the war. Left to right: Fredi, Gisel, Magda, Ferencz, Michael. In front: Michael's youngest brother, George. Budapest, 1947.

1   Michael and his friends – the "five twins" – in Budapest. Standing: Misi (left);
    Szusz (centre); and Bandi (right). Seated: Michael (left) and Pista (right). Margit
    Island, mid-1940s.

2   Michael and his brother Fredi in Paris before immigrating to Canada. Back row,
    left to right: Michael's friend Zoltan Freeman and Zoltan's brothers Hershu and
    Shiyu. Seated, left to right: Michael, Fredi and Zoltan's nephew Emil Black. Paris,
    December 1948.

3   Michael and Fredi on their first Shabbes after their arrival in Hamilton. January 1949.

4   Michael's parents, Gisel and Ferencz, and his brother George on their first day in
    Canada. Toronto, 1951.

3

1 Michael with new friends in early 1950s Hamilton. Left to right: Robert Barany, Emil Black, name unknown, Michael, and Dugyu Sternberg. In back: Jack Rosen.

2 Michael, Fredi and Robert. Hamilton, circa 1952.

3 Michael and his father, 1953.

Michael Mason, circa 1955.

Michael and Ruth (Ricky) on their wedding day. July 1954.

1   Michael with his sister, Magda, and mother, Gisel. Hamilton, early 1950s.
2   Gisel with her grandchild Robin. May 1956.
3 & 4 Gisel and Ferencz Friedman, circa 1960.

1 Michael with his wife, Ruth (Ricky), and Ricky's mother, Ray Rosenbaum. Toronto, 1957.
2 Michael and Ricky's children. In back, Robin and Andrew; in front, Tov and Roseanne. Toronto, circa 1970.
3 Left to right: Andrew, Roseanne, Robin and Tov. Late 1970s.

1 Michael and his son Andrew. Early 1980s.
2 Andrew, the day before he died. Kathmandu, Nepal, September 1983.
3 The Serious Head Injury Ward in Bir Hospital. The plaque honouring Andrew is to the right of the doorway. Kathmandu, Nepal.
4 Close-up of plaque honouring Andrew at Bir Hospital. Kathmandu, Nepal.

Michael in his denture clinic. November 1983.

Wedding of Michael and Doreen. March 7, 1987.

The Yad Vashem certificate recognizing Michael's grandson Jacob Wagner for twinning with Miklos Moskovits on the occasion of his bar mitzvah. Toronto, April 2011.

Michael holding the soapstone sculpture he made representing "Never Again."

1

2

1 A variety of the soapstone images Michael has sculpted over the years.
2 Michael's miniature sculptures from gold.

2

1

1   Michael and Doreen (far right) with Michael's sister, Magda, and brother Fredi. Chanukah, December 2014.

2   The extended Mason and Ray families celebrating Chanukah, 2014. Back row, left to right: son-in-law Robert; Doreen's daughter, Cheryl; granddaughter Sophie; daughter-in-law Lisa; grandson Adam; Michael's son, Tov; granddaughter Ruby; Michael's brother Fredi; granddaughter Zoe; son-in-law Mark; Michael's daughter Roseanne; granddaughter Sarah Rachel; granddaughter Danielle; son-in-law Frank; Danielle's boyfriend, Kevin; and daughter-in-law Marian. Middle row, left to right: Doreen; granddaughter Selma; Michael; Michael's sister, Magda; and Michael's daughter Robin. Front row, left to right: granddaughter Emily; grandson Henry; Doreen's son, Joel; grandson Cy; grandson Jacob; grandson Av; and grandson Andrew.

Michael and Doreen celebrating Michael's eightieth birthday.

Index

The Azrieli Foundation was established in 1989 to realize and extend the philanthropic vision of David J. Azrieli, C.M., C.Q., M.Arch. The Foundation's mission is to support a wide spectrum of initiatives in education and research. The Azrieli Foundation is an active supporter of programs in the fields of Education, the education of architects, scientific and medical research, and the arts. The Azrieli Foundation's many initiatives include: the Holocaust Survivor Memoirs Program, which collects, preserves, publishes and distributes the written memoirs of survivors in Canada; the Azrieli Institute for Educational Empowerment, an innovative program successfully working to keep at-risk youth in school; the Azrieli Fellows Program, which promotes academic excellence and leadership on the graduate level at Israeli universities; the Azrieli Music Project, which celebrates and fosters the creation of high-quality new Jewish orchestral music; and the Azrieli Neurodevelopmental Research Program, which supports advanced research on neurodevelopmental disorders, particularly Fragile X and Autism Spectrum Disorders.